nt **Issues**

ıter Current Issues

DISCRIMINATION
H CARE INDUSTRY

Health Law Center

Aspen Health Law Center Curre

Managed Care: State Regulation

Health Care Fraud and Abuse

Physicians as Employees

Employment Discrimination
in the Health Care Industry

Employee Benefits:
A Guide for Health Care Professionals

Aspen Health Law Center Current Issues

EMPLOYMENT DISCRIMINATION IN THE HEALTH CARE INDUSTRY

Aspen Health Law Center

AN ASPEN PUBLICATION®
Aspen Publishers, Inc.
Gaithersburg, Maryland
1998

Library of Congress Cataloging-in-Publication Data

Employment discrimination in the health care industry / Aspen Health Law Center.
        p.   cm. — (Aspen Health Law Center current issues)
                Includes bibliographical references and index.
                        ISBN 0-8342-1122-X (pbk.)
        1. Health facilities—Employees—Legal status, laws, etc.—United States.
        2. Discrimination in employment—Law and legislation—United States.
                        I. Aspen Health Law Center.   II. Series.
                                        KG3580.H4E46   1998
344.7301'133—dc21   98-9551
                                                          CIP

Orders: (800) 638-8437
Customer Service: (800) 234-1660

About Aspen Publishers • For more than 35 years, Aspen has been a leading professional publisher in a variety of disciplines. Aspen's vast information resources are available in both print and electronic formats. We are committed to providing the highest quality information available in the most appropriate format for our customers. Visit Aspen's Internet site for more information resources, directories, articles, and a searchable version of Aspen's full catalog, including the most recent publications: **http://www.aspenpub.com**
Aspen Publishers, Inc. • The hallmark of quality in publishing
Member of the worldwide Wolters Kluwer group.

Editorial Services: Brian MacDonald
Library of Congress Catalog Card Number: 98-9551
ISBN: 0-8342-1122-X

Printed in the United States of America

1   2   3   4   5

Table of Contents

Preface viii

Equal Employment Opportunity Laws..................... 1

Civil Rights Act of 1964... 1

Recent Development under Title VII............................ 4
Discrimination Based on Race 4
Discrimination Based on Sex 8
    Advertising and Preemployment Inquiries 9
    Relationship of Title VII to the
    Equal Pay Act of 1963 10
    Fringe Benefits 11
    Employment Policies Relating to Pregnancy
    and Childbirth... 12
    Grooming and Dress Code Policies 16
    Sexual Orientation.. 16
    Sexual Harassment.. 17
    Recent Developments in Sex Discrimination......... 20
        Employment Policies Related to
        Pregnancy and Childbirth 23
        Same-Gender Sexual Harassment 24
Discrimination Based on Religion 26
    Recent Developments in
    Religious Discrimination 27
Discrimination Based on National Origin 28
Reverse Discrimination.. 30
Enforcement and Remedies under Title VII.................... 31
    Recent Developments in Title VII Remedies........... 34

v

Defenses Available to the Employer 35
Notice, Reporting, and Recordkeeping 36

Equal Pay Act of 1963 .... **37**
What Is Equal Work? 38
Hospital Employees 39
Comparable Worth 41
Fringe Benefits 41
Defenses Available to the Employer 42
Enforcement and Remedies 43
Recent Developments under the Equal Pay Act 44

Age Discrimination in Employment Act **44**
Prohibited Acts... 45
Exceptions and Exemptions 48
Bona Fide Occupational Qualification 48
Reasonable Factors Other Than Age 48
Bona Fide Seniority Systems 49
Employee Benefit Plans and Mandatory
Retirement Ages 49
Exemptions 49
Enforcement and Remedies 49
Recordkeeping Requirements 51
Recent Developments under the
Age Discrimination in Employment Act 52

The Rehabilitation Act of 1973 .... **52**
Defining Disability.. 53
Who Is Otherwise Qualified? 55
Drugs and Alcohol 56
Contagious Diseases 56
Recent Developments in Defining Disability 57
Employment Practices under Section 504 60
Recent Developments in
Employment Practices 61
Reasonable Accommodation 61
Application and Interview Questions............................. 64
Notice, Reporting, and Recordkeeping 65
Enforcement and Remedies 66
Recent Developments in Remedies 67

Americans with Disabilities Act of 1990 67

Defining Disability.. 68
  Recent Developments in Defining Disability 70
  Who Is Otherwise Qualified?................................. 73
  Recent Developments in Identifying
  Who Is Otherwise Qualified 73
Reasonable Accommodations.............................. 75
Application and Interview Questions............................ 79
Insurance 80
  Recent Developments in Insurance........................ 81
Enforcement and Remedies 83
  Recent Developments in Remedies........................ 84

Civil Rights Act of 1991 86

Family and Medical Leave Act 88

Recent Developments under the Family and
Medical Leave Act 90

Conflict of Laws 91

Leave 92
Conflicting Disability Definitions 93

Employee Waivers of Discrimination Claims............. 95

Index 111

Preface

This book, *Employment Discrimination in the Health Care Industry,* is part of a collection of reference products addressing issues of current interest in the field of health care law. These products are designed to provide up-to-date, easy-to-retrieve information on a variety of topics selected on the basis of their relevance to late-breaking developments in the health care industry. The subjects covered in the inaugural group of products include *Managed Care: State Regulation, Health Care Fraud and Abuse, Physicians as Employees,* and *Employee Benefits: A Guide for Health Care Professionals.* Other topics will be added to this legal reference series as the need arises.

The books are designed to provide practical overviews of the principal legal issues relating to each topic. They are extensively footnoted, and a Table of Contents and Index provide easy access to the information. Most of the products also offer a selection of support documents, including statutory text, model contract language, and administrative rulings and guidance.

The series is compiled by the attorneys and editors on staff at the Health Law Center of Aspen Publishers, who contributed to developing these products through their writing and research efforts. We hope that these products, either separately or as a group, will meet the busy health care professional's ongoing need for information in the rapidly evolving field of health care law.

EQUAL EMPLOYMENT OPPORTUNITY LAWS

The primary focus of the Civil Rights movement, which began in the1940s, was on challenging, in the courts and legislatures, discrimination based on race. By the 1960s, however, other minority groups, observing the legal success of the attacks on racial discrimination, also began to demand protection from discrimination in the workplace. Congressional response to these demands resulted in legislation that dramatically restructured the relationship between employers and employees who are minorities and/or women. The various equal employment opportunity (EEO) laws passed by Congress have created broad classes of protected individuals. The following overview examines the most significant pieces of legislation.

CIVIL RIGHTS ACT OF 1964

Title VII of the Civil Rights Act of 1964, as amended,[1] has been described as the singularly most important part of the Act. Although many of the formerly controversial provisions of the Act, such as the right to public accommodations, are now of no more than historical interest, Title VII continues to have an important impact on the everyday employment practices of hospitals.

Briefly summarized, Title VII prohibits disparate employment treatment based on race, color, religion, sex, national origin, or pregnancy. An examination of the legislative history of Title VII reveals that although Congress viewed employment discrimination as primarily a series of isolated acts stemming from individual ill will, Title VII was designed through both its substantive and procedural aspects to remedy the problem of employment discrimination.

In 1972, Congress amended Title VII to extend its coverage.[2] The definition of employer was broadened to bring state and local governments, governmental agencies, political subdivisions, departments, and agencies within the Act's coverage.[3] Thus, since 1972, the employment practices of all hospitals—

Source: Portions reprinted from *Hospital Law Manual*, pp. Labor 1–Labor 62. © 1998, Aspen Publishers, Inc.

private, state operated, or federally operated—have been regulated by Title VII. Only religious groups and their educational institutions are exempted from the Act.[4] Under Title VII, it is an unlawful employment practice for an employer:

(1) to fail or refuse to hire or to discharge any individual, or otherwise to discriminate against any individual with respect to his or her compensation, terms, conditions, or privileges of employment, because of such individual's race, color, religion, sex, or national origin; or

(2) to limit, segregate, or classify his employees or applicants for employment in any way which would deprive or tend to deprive any individual of employment opportunities or otherwise adversely affect his status as an employee, because of such individual's race, color, religion, sex, or national origin.[5]

It is also unlawful for employers, employment agencies, and labor organizations to discriminate against protected individuals with respect to admission into a training or apprenticeship program.[6]

Other practices made unlawful by Title VII are

- discriminating against any employee or applicant who has (1) opposed practices that are illegal under Title VII or (2) filed a charge, testified, or participated in any stage of a Title VII case[7]
- advertising in any way that establishes any preference, limitation, specification, or discrimination based upon race, color, religion, sex, or national origin[8]
- discriminating in the hiring, firing, promotion, or tenure of an individual because of her pregnancy[9]

Employment discrimination is generally found under two distinct legal theories that are common to the various types of discrimination (e.g., race or sex) and are integral to an understanding of Title VII. The first theory is disparate treatment.

The disparate treatment theory of employment discrimination is conceptually the easiest to understand. Basically, employers are prohibited from treating applicants or employees in a different, or disparate, manner because of their race, color, religion, sex, or national origin. Most instances of disparate treatment involve employee discipline and discharge. These cases involve a fairly straightforward type of comparative analysis. If a work rule or employment practice is not applied in a consistent fashion, disparate treatment exists. If such treatment affects any of the groups protected by Title VII, it is a violation. To demonstrate discrimination under this theory, the charging party must prove (1) that there were differences in treatment and (2) that the employer acted out of a discriminatory motive. Specifically, if disparate treatment exists, the question becomes whether there are nondiscriminatory reasons for it.

In a Title VII disparate treatment case, the initial burden of proving discrimination is upon the complainant. Generally, once a complainant has established a prima facie case (i.e., has shown that the possibility of discrimination exists), the burden of producing evidence is imposed on the employer, who must "articulate some legitimate, nondiscriminatory reason for respondent's rejection."[10] If the employer is able to articulate such a reason, the complainant must then show that the employer's reasons are merely a pretext for discrimination. Thus, while the burden of proof shifts, it ultimately remains with the complainant. The requirements of disparate treatment are discussed further in the context of cases throughout this chapter.

A second theory of discrimination is known as disparate impact or adverse impact. Essentially, the test is whether an employer's practice, although it may appear nondiscriminatory, disproportionately affects individuals of a protected group. The classic example of an employment practice that may have an adverse impact on minorities is the use of standardized written employment tests. Although the same tests may be given to minorities and nonminorities, the minorities may not score as well and, thus, may be hired in fewer numbers than the nonminority test takers. If such a test is not job related (i.e., does not test for qualities necessary to the successful performance of the job), the employer will be found to have violated Title VII.

A charging party may attempt to establish a case by creating an inference of discrimination based upon statistical proof.

Statistics may be used, for example, to compare the percentage of minorities in an employer's work force with the percentage in the available work pool. A significant discrepancy, if unexplained, may justify a finding that the employer's practices are discriminatory. Thus, use of statistics is, in essence, the legislative version of the adage, "where there is smoke, there is fire."

Recent Development under Title VII

The U.S. Supreme Court has settled the question of how Title VII's retaliation provision applies to former employees. A discharged employee can sue his former employer under Title VII for giving a negative reference to a prospective employer, the United States Supreme Court has ruled. The employee claimed the negative reference was in retaliation for filing an Equal Employment Opportunity Commission (EEOC) charge against the employer. The employer defended that only employees are protected under Title VII, and that the former employee was not protected by the antiretaliation provision. The high court agreed to hear the case to resolve a conflict among the circuit courts. Examining the language of the statute to determine whether the term *employee* was ambiguous, the court determined that it was. The statute does not expressly refer to current employees or former employees, the Court noted. Although the context of some sections makes it clear that the legislature refers only to current employees (promotion and wage provisions, for example), other sections are more inclusive (referring to hiring and reinstatement, for example). Persuaded by the EEOC's argument that excluding former employees would undermine the purpose of Title VII by allowing employers to deter discrimination victims from filing complaints through the threat of negative references, the Court held that Title VII protects both current and former employees from retaliation. Thus, the former employee in this case could sue.[11]

Discrimination Based on Race

Title VII prohibits discriminatory practices in recruiting, hiring, advancing, firing, and setting conditions and privileges of employment that are based on race.[12] Specifically, under Title VII, employers must provide equal facilities for all employees, and may not base overtime, work assignments, or hours on the race of employees. For example, the Ninth Circuit has ruled that a Black food manager may bring a Title VII racial discrimination claim alleging he was denied the opportunity to exercise supervisory duties as contained in his job description.[13] The court stated that although the hospital was not required to allow the manager to exercise supervisory duties, to deny such responsibilities on the basis of race would violate Title VII.

Title VII's ban on discrimination based on race does not have the same meaning as discrimination based on color, also prohibited in Title VII, a federal court in Georgia has ruled.[14] Although color is usually thought to have the same meaning as race, the court found that in specifically referring to discrimination based on color in the law, Congress meant to prohibit discrimination based on color and not merely repeat its ban on racial discrimination. It is therefore possible to allege color discrimination in employment if, for example, a light-skinned Black employee is discharged by a darker-skinned Black supervisor. Color discrimination may also exist against various ethnic Caucasian groups.[15]

Title VII prohibits not only blatantly discriminatory acts, but also facially neutral employment decisions that impact members of one race more severely. Health care institutions may refute disparate impact allegations by showing that the facially neutral action was required by "business necessity."[16] The Civil Rights Act of 1991 has codified this defense as follows: Once an employee has shown that a facially neutral practice disparately impacts a protected group, to avoid liability the employer must show that the practice is job-related and consistent with business necessity.[17] An employee may still prevail, however, upon a showing that the employer refused to adopt a less discriminatory alternative.[18]

A hospital must be especially careful to avoid policies with a discriminatory effect if the institution has a history of past discrimination. For example, a state hospital in Georgia whose employment practices had a disparate impact on Blacks was found to have violated Title VII.[19] The federal court noted that after the hospital began integrating in 1965, Blacks were still not afforded the same employment opportunities as Whites. In light of the hospital's discriminatory past, and due to statistical evidence of the extensive personal discretion exercised in employment decisions and the hospital's failure to inform Blacks of available employment opportunities, the court found that the hospital's policies had a disparate, discriminatory impact on Blacks.

Disparate impact cases can arise from a variety of seemingly neutral personnel policies. If an employee can establish that such policies have the effect of limiting the number of Blacks or minorities employed by the hospital, the employer may be held liable for discrimination. For example, policies that have possible discriminatory ramifications are those in which an employer regularly hires largely through word-of-mouth or in which an employer hires relatives of current employees.[20] In addition, an employer's job promotions based on not clearly job-related written examinations and having a disparate impact on Blacks constitutes racial discrimination and cannot be justified because the "bottom line" of the employer's promotional process achieves an appropriate racial balance.[21] A hospital should consider the ramifications of the failure to hire or the discharge of an employee based solely on his or her arrest or conviction record, also.[22] Additional employment practices that may discriminate against certain minorities include consideration of an individual's poor credit rating, discharge of an employee whose wages are garnished or who is an unwed mother, and the non–job-related requirement of a high school diploma. Hospitals should carefully monitor their application, grievance, and discharge policies. Employment application forms should request as little race-specific information as possible to avoid a racially disproportionate impact. Layoff criteria that adversely affects both Black and White hospital employees has been held nondiscriminatory, however.[23]

The hospital must be aware of any business necessities that can serve as a defense to a claim of discrimination based on race. For example, a hospital that moves from an inner-city location to an outlying suburban area may be charged with discrimination because the total number of minority employees decreases significantly.[24] However, the hospital could rebut such a charge by producing evidence of the poor financial condition of the hospital at the old site, the decline in its usage, and the need for the hospital in the suburbs. Such a defense would constitute business necessity.

The Civil Rights Act of 1866 is a second source of racial discrimination litigation. This Act, more commonly known by its United States Code designations, Section 1981 and Section 1982, was passed to effectuate the Thirteenth Amendment to the U.S. Constitution, which outlawed slavery. Section 1981 provides that:

> [a]ll persons within the jurisdiction of the United States shall have the same right in every State and Territory to make and enforce contracts . . . as is enjoyed by white citizens. . . .[25]

Although Section 1981 is more than 100 years old, federal courts have come to recognize only recently that it bars racial discrimination in employment.

The Supreme Court has reviewed the relationship between Section 1981 and Title VII, and held that the former "affords a federal remedy against discrimination in private employment on the basis of race" independent of the remedy provided for by Title VII.[26]

Section 1981 is also significant because the time limit for bringing a complaint of discrimination may be considerably longer than the 180-day limit set in Title VII. The Supreme Court has held that the time limit for filing a complaint is determined by the most analogous state law.[27] Section 1981 is also significant in that some courts have held it to forbid discrimination against aliens in employment.[28] The Supreme Court has held that Title VII does not forbid such discrimination.[29]

Finally, the U.S. Supreme Court has also ruled that certain non-Black ethnic groups may bring racial discrimination suits under 42 U.S.C. § 1981 and 1982. The Court reached this conclusion in two separate cases in which federal courts had ruled that these laws do not pertain to discrimination based on ancestry.[30]

Discrimination Based on Sex

The prohibition under Title VII against discrimination based on sex applies equally to males and females.[31] Sex discrimination complaints have been filed by men who have been denied access to jobs traditionally thought of in the health care industry as "women's jobs" (i.e., nursing). The EEOC has issued comprehensive guidelines on most of the issues related to sex discrimination.[32]

If a hospital can demonstrate that sex "is a bona fide occupational qualification reasonably necessary to the normal operation" of its business, the general prohibition against gender bias under Title VII will be waived.[33] A federal court in Michigan, for example, ruled that sex can be a bona fide occupational qualification (BFOQ) for mental health care workers because same-gender caretakers are required to protect the privacy rights of mentally ill patients.[34] The EEOC, however, continues to interpret the BFOQ exception in an extremely limited manner. Therefore, assumptions based on employment characteristics of women; stereotypical characteristics based on sex; and preferences of employers, coworkers, or clients generally are not considered BFOQs.[35]

The hospital cannot merely assert that patients prefer one gender or the other to provide patient care. Numerous cases have rejected nursing home and hospital contentions that patients prefer one gender over the other.[36] A hospital may successfully defend a gender discrimination suit, however, by proving that sex is a BFOQ. One facility escaped liability by proving that female gender was a BFOQ for labor and delivery nurses, for example.[37]

A hospital that replaces a discharged female employee with another female employee may still be charged with sex discrimination.[38] Although the sex of an employee's replacement may be relevant to the inquiry, it does not alone determine whether the circumstances suggest discrimination. Similarly, a discharged nurse was not prevented from suing for sex discrimination when the decision to discharge the nurse was made by a woman and the position filled by another woman several months later.[39] Managers of all genders and races may feel that action against a disfavored group will be less controversial, the court observed, and managers who are themselves members of a disfavored group may feel pressured to demonstrate their ability to sanction members of their own group.

In the past, many states enacted legislation designed to "protect" women from certain "onerous" job responsibilities. Such state laws may have forbidden the employment of women in certain jobs; limited the hours, days, or time of day during which women may work; prohibited the employment of women in jobs that required lifting or carrying weights over specified limits; and/or controlled the employment of women during pregnancy or after childbirth. Often, special rest and meal periods or special facilities were required for women.

A hospital cannot excuse itself from the mandate of Title VII merely by showing that it complies with a state law or regulation.[40] The EEOC guidelines indicate, and the courts continue to hold, that Title VII supersedes state laws and regulations.[41] The touchstone of Title VII is that all job applicants and employees must be judged by their individual abilities and preferences rather than by the sexual stereotypes embodied in state protective laws and regulations.

Hospitals must base employment decisions on job-related factors. If a hospital refuses to hire married women, it cannot hire married men. Institutional policies prohibiting the hiring of a spouse of a current employee have been held by a federal appeals court not to discriminate against women.[42] The particular rule examined by the court did not require the discharge of either spouse already married when the policy was promulgated, however, nor did it apply to an employee who married another employee. Moreover, state laws are often more stringent than federal laws. Because the alleged discriminatee has the option of pursuing her claim under the federal or state system (or both), hospitals must keep abreast of current developments at the state level.

Advertising and Preemployment Inquiries
EEOC guidelines relating to advertising prohibit the use of employment opportunity columns headed "male" or "female."[43] Although an employer is free under Title VII to inquire about

the sex of a prospective employee, it is unwise for a health care institution to ask such a question on its employment application unless there is clear evidence that such a question is not intended to limit hiring based on an individual's sex.[44]

Evidence that an employer asked family-oriented questions only of a female job applicant is not sufficient to support a claim of intentional sex discrimination, the Seventh Circuit has ruled.[45] An employer who was hiring for a paramedic position asked a female applicant how many children she had, whether it was time to have more children, what she had arranged for child care, and how her husband felt about her working 24-hour shifts. Acknowledging that these questions were based on sex stereotypes, the court ruled that the woman must still prove that the employer relied on her gender in making his decision to hire a male for the position. In this case, the employer demonstrated that he was concerned about the family circumstances of any applicant where both husband and wife work 24-hour shifts. In addition, the employer indicated that he had resolved his concerns with respect to the woman applicant because he had written on her application form that child care was not a problem. Because the woman could not rebut the employer's nondiscriminatory reasons for hiring a male, the court dismissed the woman's suit.

Relationship of Title VII to the Equal Pay Act of 1963

Until the 1980s, the courts had relatively few problems interpreting the interrelationship between Title VII and the Equal Pay Act of 1963. The Equal Pay Act applied to wage disparities between the sexes and required equal pay for equal work. Title VII allowed an employer to pay different wages to male and female employees as long as the work they performed was not equal. Title VII did, however, apply to disparate levels of fringe benefits.

In the 1980s, the courts began to accept a new theory, known as comparable worth, that greatly affected the relationship between Title VII and the Equal Pay Act. In brief, under the comparable worth theory, Title VII covers situations in which "women's jobs" are undervalued simply because they are held primarily by women.

In 1981, the U.S. Supreme Court, skirting the concept of "comparable worth," ruled that female employees may bring sex-based wage discrimination suits under Title VII of the Civil Rights Act of 1964 without showing that male coworkers perform substantially equal work for higher pay.[46] The Court focused on whether the Bennett amendment, an amendment to Title VII that bars sex-based wage discrimination unless "authorized" by the Equal Pay Act, also incorporates that Act's "equal work" requirement as a condition for bringing suit. Concluding that such a requirement is not part of Title VII, the Supreme Court explained that if that position were adopted, women would be barred from suing for even the most egregious discrimination unless they could show that they did exactly the same work as higher-paid men.

Fringe Benefits

Fringe benefits are defined by the EEOC guidelines as "medical, hospital, accident, life insurance and retirement benefits, profit sharing and bonus plans, [and] leave."[47] Fringe benefits must be granted equally to men and women. The hospital that provides benefits for the wives of male employees and not for the husbands of female employees, or benefits for the husbands of female employees and not for the wives of male employees, is in violation of Title VII.[48] One federal court has ruled, however, that a company's policy of including spouses in employee medical insurance coverage only if the employee earns more than the spouse did not violate Title VII because it served the legitimate business purpose of keeping the cost of the plan low and providing coverage for the neediest employees.[49] The Supreme Court has rejected a similar distinction, ruling in 1983 that an employer's health insurance plan that provides less favorable pregnancy benefits for spouses of male employees than for female employees constitutes sex discrimination against the male employees.[50] Institutions should note, however, that Title VII does not require an employer to carry separate medical policies for employees who are husband and wife; it requires only equal treatment and benefits. Further, EEOC guidelines prohibit an employer from setting different mandatory or optional retirement ages and from providing different retirement or pension benefits based on sex.[51] The U.S. Supreme Court has approved this by ruling that a retirement plan that pays women lower monthly benefits than men when both have made the same dollar contributions to the plan is illegal sex discrimination.[52]

Discharging a female employee because of the high medical costs her infant child was expected to incur does not constitute discrimination on the basis of sex, however, the U.S. Court of Appeals for the Sixth Circuit has ruled.[53] After she was discharged, the nurse sued for sex discrimination under the Pregnancy Discrimination Act (PDA) of 1978, an amendment to Title VII.[54] The Sixth Circuit ruled that the reason for the nurse's discharge was the company's desire to avoid the high future medical costs associated with the illness of her child, which would be paid by the company's self-insurance plan. The court held that this was not related to the nurse's gender or pregnancy, and was therefore not illegal under Title VII. Actions taken with regard to a child are not equivalent to "action because of or on the basis of" her pregnancy, the court ruled. The law's reference to "women affected by . . . related medical conditions" refers to related conditions of the pregnant woman, the court explained, not conditions of the offspring.

Employment Policies Relating to Pregnancy and Childbirth

The PDA amendment to Title VII prohibits discriminatory treatment of pregnant women for all employment-related purposes, including hiring, promotion, and levels of fringe benefits. It affirms the prior EEOC position that an employer who fails to hire and promote or fires a woman solely because she is pregnant violates Title VII. Indeed, if an employment practice has an adverse effect upon pregnant women, even if unintentional, an employer must be able to show business necessity to justify the practice.

The U.S. Supreme Court has ruled on the validity of a fetal protection policy in *International Union v. Johnson Controls, Inc.*,[55] finding that a company's policy to bar fertile women from battery-making jobs involving exposure to lead violates Title VII. The company argued that the safety of unconceived fetuses in jobs involving lead exposure is an instance where gender is a BFOQ, and the policy therefore embodies permissible discrimination under Title VII. The Court ruled, however, that the BFOQ defense has a very narrow scope and does not transform concern for the safety of fetuses into an essential aspect of battery-making. The Court also concluded that sex was not an occupational qualification in this case, noting that fertile women participate in the manufacture of batteries as efficiently as anyone else.

In response to the U.S. Supreme Court's ruling in *United Auto Workers v. Johnson Controls*, the EEOC has issued a policy guide to assist its investigators in determining whether fetal protection policies violate Title VII of the 1964 Civil Rights Act.[56] Although policy guides do not carry the weight of a regulation, hospitals should be familiar with policy guides, because they establish an agency's position with regard to specific issues. The fetal protection policy states that as a result of the Supreme Court's ruling, policies that exclude members of one sex from a workplace for the purpose of protecting fetuses cannot be justified under Title VII. Accordingly, the EEOC states, a complaint alleging that an employer excludes members of only one sex from employment based on a fetal protection policy should be pursued. The fact that an employer can prove that a substance to which its workers are exposed will endanger the health of a fetus or that an employer will incur a higher cost if hiring women is irrelevant, according to the policy. Individuals who can perform the essential functions of a job must be considered eligible for employment, regardless of the presence of workplace hazards to fetuses.

A decision not to hire a female applicant based solely on her status as an unwed mother has been found to constitute a violation of Title VII.[57] Even if an institution claims to apply a similar policy to men with illegitimate children, courts have responded that, because it is easier for a man to hide the fact that he has an illegitimate child than it is for a woman, such a policy can never be applied equally; therefore, such a policy necessarily has a greater effect on women than on men.[58]

At one time, pregnancy had its greatest impact on hospitals in the area of maternity leave for its employees. The Family and Medical Leave Act (discussed below) now requires employers to grant job-protected leave for parents upon the birth of a child. Health care employers must continue to ensure, however, that policies relating to leave because of pregnancy are similar to those for other types of disability leaves. For example, a federal trial court ruled that a nursing home's leave of absence policy that imposed a three-month limit on maternity leave, but permitted an indefinite leave of absence for illness other than pregnancy, violated the PDA amendment to Title VII.[59] Arbitrarily determined mandatory maternity leaves not based on ability or inability to work violate Title VII. Mandatory leaves based on the inability to work are permitted, however. Therefore, an employer was found not to have committed illegal sex-based discrimination when it placed a pregnant worker on involuntary maternity leave because she could not perform the lifting requirements of her job.[60]

According to the EEOC guidelines, an employer's decision to terminate an employee who is temporarily disabled due to pregnancy violates the PDA if the termination is the result of an insufficient leave policy that has a disparate impact on females and is not justified by business necessity.[61] The Seventh Circuit has confirmed that employees who challenge maternity leave under the PDA amendments to Title VII may rely on the theory of disparate impact.[62] The court observed that the PDA changed the definition of discrimination based on sex, but did not change the substantive rules of Title VII for assessing discrimination. Because both disparate treatment and practices with disparate impact are forbidden under Title VII's general provisions, pregnancy discrimination charges should also be assessed under the disparate impact approach of Title VII.

Pregnancy is not considered a disability per se. It is only when pregnant workers become disabled that benefits must be paid. Employers should remember that the PDA allows them to require a physician's certification that the pregnant employee is unable to work. Further, an employer may also require a company physician's confirmation of the medical disability as long as such requirements are uniformly required of all employees who seek disability or sick leave.

An employer who does not provide paid sick leave or disability benefits to other employees should review personnel records to determine whether the failure to provide leave or benefits has a disparate impact on female employees due to pregnancy.[63]

The Family and Medical Leave Act of 1993 directly addresses the issue of maternity (and paternity) leave.[64] The law was enacted, in part, because of Congress's perception that employment standards applicable to only one gender have a serious potential for encouraging employers to discriminate against employees and job applicants of that gender. Under the law, an eligible employee is entitled because of the birth of a child to 12 workweeks of unpaid leave during any 12-month period to care for the child. Several states have also enacted legislation requiring employers to grant a minimum leave of absence for pregnancy, and the aforementioned analysis must be read together with individual state requirements. The U.S. Supreme Court has ruled, for example, that a California statute that requires employers to provide pregnant employees with unpaid leave and reinstatement to their former jobs is not preempted by the 1978 PDA amendments to Title VII.[65]

After enactment of the PDA in 1978, federal courts differed on whether an employer who offers health insurance coverage for an employee's spouse is required to provide coverage for the spouse's pregnancy-related illnesses. For example, several courts held that the PDA did not require that pregnancy benefits for employees' spouses be equivalent to other disability benefits provided to spouses. In *Newport News Shipbuilding & Dry Dock Co. v. EEOC*[66] the Fourth Circuit held, however, that the PDA requires employers to treat pregnancy-related disability in the same manner as other disabilities. In 1983, the Supreme Court upheld the Fourth Circuit opinion, ruling that under the PDA, it is discriminatory to exclude pregnancy coverage for employees' spouses from an otherwise inclusive benefit plan. To do so would unlawfully give married male employees a less inclusive benefits package for their dependents than the dependents' coverage provided to married female employees, the Court concluded.[67] Employers are not prevented from treating pregnancy more beneficially than other disabilities, however, the Sixth Circuit has ruled, rejecting an employer's attempt to use *Newport News* as justification for imposing a preexisting coverage provision on pregnancy claims, although not specifically required to do so under the policy.[68] Further, at least one court has applied the *Newport News* rationale retroactively to the date of passage of the PDA.[69]

Grooming and Dress Code Policies

Title VII does not prohibit an employer from making an employment decision based upon factors such as grooming and dress. Numerous court decisions have upheld the employer's right to require men to have short haircuts[70] or to wear ties,[71] and women to wear dresses.[72] The courts have reasoned that, because dress code and grooming policies are more closely related to an employer's choice of how to run the business than to the employer's obligation to provide equal employment opportunities, such a stance is justified.[73]

A U.S. Court of Appeals decision, however, indicates that dress codes will be subjected to a different standard of scrutiny in those instances in which male and female employees who perform the same functions are expected to conform to two entirely different dress codes.[74] This decision, however, by no means disposes of this issue. Indeed, one court has gone so far as to state that employees can choose to accept or reject the employer's policy.[75] If they choose to reject the grooming or dress policy, they are subject to the sanctions imposed by the employer.

Sexual Orientation

Court opinions indicate that Title VII does not protect employees who allege discrimination on the basis of sexual preference. Courts have held that a company's refusal to hire an effeminate male does not constitute sex discrimination under Title VII.[76] In a related case, a court held that a hospital did not violate Title VII by discharging an employee who intended to have a sex change operation.[77]

Sexual Harassment

The area of sexual harassment in the workplace has taken on increasing importance. In the wake of the well-publicized investigation of sexual harassment allegations against then Supreme Court nominee Clarence Thomas, sexual harassment claims are on the rise. Health care institutions should be particularly sensitive to the potential for liability, due to the large numbers of female health care employees.

Sexual harassment is prohibited by Title VII.[78] Unwelcome sexual advances, requests for sexual favors, and other verbal or physical conduct of a sexual nature constitute sexual harassment when submission to such conduct is a term or condition of employment, submission to such conduct becomes the basis for employment-related decisions, or such conduct unreasonably interferes with an employee's job performance or creates a hostile or intimidating work environment.[79]

There are two types of sexual harassment: quid pro quo and hostile environment harassment. Quid pro quo harassment occurs when submission to unwelcome sexual advances, requests for sexual favors, and other verbal or physical conduct of a sexual nature becomes the basis for employment-related decisions. To prove quid pro quo harassment, the employee must show that sexual advances were made, the advances were unwelcome, and the harasser threatened or implemented retaliation for rejection of advances.

An employee who sues on a quid pro quo theory of sexual harassment need not prove actual economic harm, according to a federal appeals court.[80] A university employee who worked in a fundraising office entered into a sexual relationship with her supervisor. She claimed she began the relationship under coercion and that her employment raises, hours, autonomy, and flexibility varied, depending on her responsiveness to her supervisor's sexual advances. She later brought a sexual harassment suit against the university, based on a quid pro quo theory. The university argued that the employee could not recover because she suffered no economic injury, as she had received raises and promotions during the alleged harassment. The employee responded that economic injury is not a prerequisite of a quid pro quo sexual harassment suit. The Second Circuit agreed with the employee, ruling that although employees who reject employers' sexual advances are often able to show economic injury in a quid pro quo suit, such a showing is not required. To require employees to show actual, rather than threatened, economic loss would improperly condition recovery on the employee's reaction to the prohibited conduct, rather than on the conduct itself, the court reasoned.

Hostile environment harassment occurs when the conduct creates a hostile or intimidating work environment to the degree that it interferes with an individual's ability to accomplish job tasks. To prove hostile environment harassment, the employee typically shows that conduct of a sexual nature occurred in the workplace, the conduct was unwanted, the conduct was repeated and pervasive, and the hostile environment either interfered with the employee's ability to do the job or made the job more difficult or severe.

The U.S. Supreme Court has ruled that for a claim of hostile environment sex discrimination to be actionable under Title VII of the Civil Rights Act of 1964, it must be sufficiently severe or pervasive to alter the conditions of the victim's employment and create an abusive working environment.[81] The high court has since clarified that an employee who sues her employer under Title VII for sex discrimination need not prove that she sustained tangible psychological injury to recover.[82] A female manager of an equipment rental company sued the company's president, who had suggested that the manager accompany him to a hotel to negotiate her raise and asked the manager whether she had granted sexual favors to a customer in return for business. The trial court dismissed the case, holding that the manager could not recover because she did not suffer psychological injury. The manager appealed to the Supreme Court.

The Supreme Court rejected the view that employees must show serious psychological injury, thereby resolving a split among the circuits regarding what an employee must prove to recover for sex discrimination in the workplace. It held that psychological harm is one of many factors that courts should consider to determine whether the alleged conduct created a hostile work environment. Courts must also consider other factors such as the frequency and severity of the discriminatory conduct, whether the conduct is physically threatening or humiliating, and whether it unreasonably interferes with the employee's work performance. The failure to prove any single factor, including psychological injury, will not prevent the employee from recovering under Title VII. Because the manager could recover in the absence of tangible psychological injury, the Supreme Court ordered the trial court to reconsider the case.

An employee suing for sexual harassment need not prove that the abusive conduct was exclusive to one gender, but should prove that the conduct more adversely affected one gender than the other. A cardiologist accused of sexually harassing a cardiology technician may not escape liability by arguing that his conduct was abusive to employees of both sexes, a federal appeals court has ruled.[83] The cardiologist was accused of yelling at the technician; throwing a stethoscope at her; and grabbing her by the lapels of her scrub jacket, her bra straps, and her skin, and shaking her. The technician filed a formal complaint with the hospital administration, and later sued the cardiologist and the hospital, claiming hostile environment sexual harassment. A lower court dismissed the case, ruling that there was insufficient evidence that the conduct was gender based. It pointed out that although the physician had been abusive to several female employees, he had also been abusive to male employees.

The Eighth Circuit, however, found sufficient evidence of sexual harassment to permit the case to proceed. The court noted that the incidents of abuse, spanning several years, involved primarily women, and that the incidents involving women were of a more serious nature than those involving men. It found that a fact-finder could certainly conclude that the physician's treatment of women was worse than his treatment of men. The court observed that the acts that support a hostile environment sexual harassment claim do not have to be explicitly sexual in nature. Instead, the issue is whether members of one sex are exposed to disadvantageous terms or conditions of employment to which members of the other sex are not exposed.

According to EEOC guidelines, an employer is liable for the sexual harassment of employees by supervisory and managerial staff.[84] In addition, an employer is liable for the sexual harassment of employees by coworkers or nonemployees if the employer knew of, or should have known of, such actions. In 1988, the EEOC also issued a document entitled Policy Guidance on Current Issues of Sexual Harassment. This document provides guidance in determining whether sexual conduct is unwelcome, evaluating evidence of harassment, determining whether a work environment is sexually hostile, holding employers liable for sexual harassment by supervisors, and evaluating preventive and remedial action taken in response to claims of sexual harassment.

Courts have addressed the liability of health care employers for the sexually discriminatory acts of their employees. A hospital was not liable for sexual harassment because its response to complaints of sexual harassment from a histotechnologist against the supervisor of the pathology laboratory was adequate, a federal trial court in Alabama has ruled.[85] The court noted that the hospital promptly investigated the complaint, instructed the supervisor to amend his behavior, and made adjustments in the histotechnologist's schedule so that she would not have to interact with him. In addition, the court observed, the hospital promptly investigated charges that the supervisor had threatened the histotechnologist with retaliation, and warned him that any future threats of retaliation would result in termination.[86]

Recent Developments in Sex Discrimination

The following recent cases illustrate the scope of impermissible behavior and employer liability:

- An anesthesiology resident is entitled to a trial on her claims against a hospital for sexual harassment, even though the department chair who allegedly harassed her did not make sexually explicit or threatening comments, the Eighth Circuit has ruled. The resident alleged that the department chair referred to female residents by their first names while calling male residents "Doctor," told other physicians that he had selected the female residents as "anesthesia babes," asked her why she did not become a nurse, and told her that women should be home nursing babies. The resident sued the hospital for hostile environment sexual harassment. The trial court ruled that the resident could not recover, due to the absense of sexually explicit comments and their nonthreatening nature. The appeals court reversed trial court ruling and allowed the resident to proceed. Comments need not be explicitly sexual, the court ruled. Rather the key is whether the unwelcome conduct was targeted at members of one sex but not the other.[87]

- A nursing home was not liable for a janitor's sexual harassment of a dietary aide, because the facility responded to the aide's complaints in a prompt and appropriate manner. When the aide first complained that the janitor had kissed, tickled, and hugged her and declared that he was "falling in love," the facility found no witnesses to the alleged behavior, but moved the janitor's work area, formed an "observation network" to detect further trouble, asked the aide daily whether any problems had occurred, and walked her to her car each night. When the aide complained of an additional incident, and a second aide also complained of harassment by the janitor, the facility issued a warning to the janitor that any further occurrence would result in termination. A few days later, the first aide complained that the janitor "kept coming around her," but that no specific incident had occurred. The chief administrator said she could not guarantee that the aide could work without coming into contact with the janitor. The aide resigned and sued the facility for hostile environment sexual harassment under Title VII. When presented with allegations of hostile environment sexual harassment by a coworker, an employer must institute prompt and appropriate corrective action, the court found. The employer will not be liable for the imputed acts of the coworker but rather on the basis of his own actions, the court clarified. Liability will be imposed only if the employer's response to the alleged harassment is so indifferent that it indicates permissiveness that amounts to discrimination. In this case, the employer implemented several steps to curtail the alleged harassment, acted promptly, and acted in good faith. Under the circumstances, the nursing facility was not liable.[88]

- The United States Court of Appeals for the Fifth Circuit affirmed a trial court ruling of hostile work environment sexual harassment in violation of Title VII. The plaintiff was a nurse employed by the nursing home. Nursing home administrators attributed the nurse's large number of children to a great deal of sexual activity, ignorance of birth control, and asked the nurse's coworkers about her sexual activity. The Fifth Circuit affirmed the trial court's decision that the nurse had demonstrated that she is in a protected group, that she was the subject of unwanted sexual harassment, that the harassment was sexually oriented, that the harassment was so severe as to affect her working conditions, and that management knew about the harassment.[89]

- The United States Court of Appeals for the Eleventh Circuit affirmed a trial court's holding that an employer is not liable under Title VII for sexual harassment when supervisors who harass an individual do it for their own benefit that is unconnected to their supervisory status. Nor may they be held liable for harassment when it is not proven that the employer had actual knowledge of the harassment or that the hostile environment was so pervasive so as to establish constructive knowledge.[90]

- Reversing a trial court decision, the Tenth Circuit held that an employer can be held responsible for a supervisor's sexual harassment when the supervisor has control over the victim's working environment and the supervisor's ability to harass the victim is aided by such control.[91]

- Two federal circuit courts have held that discriminatory behavior does not have to be "egregious" to award punitive damages. The Second and District of Columbia Circuits held that "garden variety" discrimination is sufficient to award punitive damages because the proof required to demonstrate discrimination, "malice or reckless indifference," was the same level necessary to award punitive damages under other federal civil rights statutes.[92]

- A psychiatric hospital that treats emotionally disturbed and sexually abused children and adolescents may require female and male staff members on all shifts, the Third Circuit has ruled, because sex is a bona fide occupational qualification.[93] A female child care specialist was assigned to the night shift in accordance with a psychiatric hospital's policy of scheduling both males and females on all shifts to satisfy the therapeutic needs and privacy concerns of its young patients. The specialist sued, arguing that the hospital discriminated against her on the basis of sex in violation of Title VII of the Civil Rights Act by assigning her to the night shift because of her gender. The federal appeals court ruled in favor of the hospital, finding that, although the hospital's policy was facially discriminatory, the policy is justified because gender is a BFOQ for child care specialists at the facility.

Employment Policies Relating to Pregnancy and Childbirth. A job requirement that nurses in a hospital's postpartum and newborn nursery unit be able to lift 150 pounds may constitute sex discrimination, a federal appeals court has ruled.[94] A pregnant nurse who took two months of medical leave at the beginning of her pregnancy sought to return to work. The hospital required the nurse's physician to fill out a form certifying that the nurse could perform all job requirements, including lifting up to 150 pounds. The physician did not approve the lifting requirement, and the hospital refused to allow the nurse to return to work, citing its policy prohibiting employees from returning from medical leave with any medical restrictions. The nurse sued, arguing that the lifting requirement was not a bona fide job duty. The disparate impact of the policies on pregnant employees, the nurse contended, violated the PDA, an amendment to Title VII's ban on sex discrimination. The court agreed that the nurse could prove disparate impact if the lifting requirement was not a genuine job duty.

The prohibition on employment discrimination because of sex in Title VII covers not only an employee's right to have an abortion but also mere contemplation of abortion, according to the Sixth Circuit.[95] A pregnant employee was fired from a hotel's staff because her consideration of having an abortion caused a controversy in the workplace. The employee sued, arguing that her discharge constituted sex discrimination under the PDA. The trial court agreed, finding that the employee's consideration of abortion was a motivating factor in her discharge and that she suffered economic and emotional injury.

The federal appeals court upheld the trial court and affirmed judgment in favor of the employee. The PDA states that discrimination because of sex includes discrimination on the basis of pregnancy and related medical conditions, the court explained. Citing the legislative history of the PDA, guidelines of the EEOC, and previous Supreme Court decisions, the Sixth Circuit determined that pregnancy-related medical conditions include the right to an abortion.

A hospital that fired a pregnant nurse who refused to treat a human immunodeficiency virus (HIV)-positive patient did not discriminate on the basis of sex, a federal appeals court has ruled.[96] When a nurse, who was in the first trimester of pregnancy, was asked to attend an HIV-positive patient with meningitis, the nurse refused to treat the patient, citing the risk that opportunistic diseases would be transmitted to her fetus. The hospital discharged the nurse, in accordance with a hospital policy, stating that refusal to treat a patient is grounds for termination. The nurse sued under Title VII, arguing that her discharge constituted discrimination on the basis of sex.

The Eleventh Circuit rejected the nurse's arguments and ruled that the hospital had not violated Title VII. Although discrimination on the basis of pregnancy is equivalent to sex discrimination, the court noted, the nurse did not prove that the hospital policy disproportionately impacted pregnant employees, as the only other nurse who resigned as a result of the policy was not pregnant.

Same-Gender Sexual Harassment. Federal appeals courts are divided as to whether Title VII permits suits for same-gender sexual harassment in the workplace, focusing on what "because of sex" or "based on sex" means. The Fourth Circuit, for example, has refused recovery for sexual harassment under Title VII where the employee claiming harassment and the alleged harassers are heterosexuals of the same sex.[97] The same court later permitted a same-gender sexual harassment suit under Title VII, where a heterosexual male alleged hostile environment sexual harassment by a group of homosexual males.[98] The Eighth Circuit has also ruled that a male employee could sue for sexual harassment under Title VII based on the conduct of his male coworkers.[99]

At least one court has continued to reject same-sex harassment claims, however. The Fifth Circuit has stated that "harassment by a male supervisor against a male subordinate does not state a claim under Title VII, even though the harassment has sexual overtones."[100] The Fifth Circuit has held that same-sex sexual harassment is not cognizable under Title VII, stating that its finding was predicated upon an internal circuit rule that prevented a panel of the Fifth Circuit from overruling an earlier panel's decision, even if it disagreed with the earlier panel's decision.[101]

In recent years, greater attention has been paid to same-sex harassment and whether sexual harassment laws, including Title VII, apply to such claims. The following cases illustrate the current path of the law and significant decisions.

- Reversing a trial court summary judgment order, the Eleventh Circuit held that Title VII actions can apply to same-sex harassment cases, because the plaintiff had made an initial showing that the harassment had occurred "because of sex."[102]

- The Supreme Judicial Court of Massachusetts has held that lewd and sexually oriented talk and behavior can violate state sexual harassment law, even when the conduct occurs between men.[103]

- A male may sue his former employer for hostile environment sexual harassment based on the conduct of a homosexual male employee who made sexual propositions and remarks, the Sixth Circuit has ruled.[104]

Discrimination Based on Religion

Employees or job applicants who claim religious discrimination must demonstrate that they are compelled by a sincere and meaningful belief to observe religious practices. Once an employee has established this, the burden shifts to the employer to demonstrate that the employee cannot be accommodated without undue hardship to the employer.[105] An employer must make some attempt to accommodate an employee's religious beliefs, the Fourth Circuit has ruled in a non–health care case, even if the employee flatly refuses to work on Sundays.[106] The U.S. Supreme Court has ruled, however, that an employer's duty to reasonably accommodate the religious beliefs of its employees does not require the employer to adopt the accommodation preferred by an employee.[107] In hospital settings, courts differ as to whether particular accommodations impose an undue hardship on employers. For example, on the one hand, one court held that it would not be an undue hardship for a hospital to accommodate a nurse's religious belief that precluded her from assisting in abortions.[108] On the other hand, because a hospital would incur substantial costs in overtime for other nurses or suffer decreased efficiency by rearranging a work schedule to accommodate a nurse's religious beliefs that forbade Saturday work, the hospital was justified in terminating her employment.[109] In a non–health care case, a federal appeals court ruled that an employer did not reasonably accommodate an employee's religious objections to working on Sunday by requiring the employee to swap shifts with other employees.[110] The court held that although it is generally sufficient to permit shift swapping, when an employee sincerely believes that it is morally wrong to induce another to work on Sunday, the employer is obligated to take further steps to accommodate that employee's religious beliefs.

In a 1987 case, the U.S. Supreme Court ruled that Florida's refusal to pay unemployment compensation to an employee who was discharged because of her religious beliefs unconstitutionally burdened the employee's right to the free exercise of her religion.[111] When a state denies a benefit because of conduct required by religious beliefs, thereby pressuring individuals to modify their behavior and violate their beliefs, the state has placed an unconstitutional burden on the free exercise of religion, the Court concluded.

Religious organizations are exempt in both their religious and secular activities from Title VII's prohibition of discrimination based on religion.[112] This is true even if such a hospital receives federal funds through Medicare payments for patient treatment, a federal court in Kansas has ruled.[113] Some doubt exists, however, about the constitutionality of the exemption as it applies to the nonreligious profit-making activities of religious groups (e.g., operating a hospital).[114] Although religious organizations may be able to discriminate in favor of members of their own faith, these employers are not immune from liability for employment discrimination based on race, sex, or national origin, or for retaliatory actions against employees who exercise their lawfully recognized rights.[115]

The Supreme Court in *Trans World Airlines, Inc. v. Hardison*[116] determined that employers and unions are not required to take steps inconsistent with the contractual seniority system to accommodate the religious practices of an employee who refused to work on Saturdays. The Court found that Congress did not intend that an employer must "deny the shift and job preferences of some employees, as well as deprive them of their contractual rights, in order to accommodate or prefer the religious needs of others." The Court appears to hold that anything more than a "de minimus" or negligible cost to the employer would constitute an "undue hardship."

Recent Developments in Religious Discrimination

On August 14, 1997, President Clinton issued executive branch guidelines for civilian employees designed to protect the exercise of religion in the federal workplace.[117] The guidelines are designed to allow greater religious expression while at work, prevent discrimination based on religious exercises, and allow "reasonable accommodation" of religious practices while at work.

The guidelines address several examples of how employers must tolerate religious behavior and practices in the workplace, including:

- keeping religious texts on the desk and reading them during breaks
- prohibiting religious posters in common areas
- allowing employees to discuss religious issues, provided that discussions do not result in evangelical behavior
- allowing employees to wear religious medallions over their clothes

Discrimination Based on National Origin

The concept of national origin as it is used in Title VII has been broadly interpreted in EEOC guidelines.[118] Discrimination based on the places of origin of persons or their ancestors or possession of identifiable characteristics of a national origin group is prohibited. Discriminatory consideration of national origin may arise from focusing on language, surname, religious or social affiliations, or membership in any organization associated with a national origin group. Although the EEOC guidelines indicate that discrimination based on the citizenship of an employee or applicant is prohibited by Title VII,[119] the Supreme Court has indicated that an employer is free to discriminate against alien applicants.[120] Some states prohibit the employment of nonresident aliens. In those states, hospitals should include a question on their employment application asking whether an applicant is a citizen of the United States and, if not, whether the applicant has a valid work permit.[121]

The EEOC has also indicated that the following types of overt and covert national origin discrimination are prohibited: (1) the use by hospitals of tests in English where the English language is not a BFOQ;[122] (2) the denial of employment or job advancement to, or firing of, people who marry or associate with people of a specific national origin or whose name indicates national origin;[123] and (3) the denial of employment or job advancement to, or firing of, individuals who seek to "promote the interests of national groups."[124]

Requiring employees to speak only English in the workplace may also lead to Title VII litigation, although employees have been unsuccessful in three recent suits. A hospital did not violate Title VII's ban on discrimination on the basis of national origin by adopting a rule prohibiting the use of Tagalog, a native language of the Philippines, by Filipina nurses during the evening shift in one of its units, a federal trial court in California has ruled.[125] The hospital argued that it had adopted the rule because the Filipina nurses' use of the language interfered with the other nurses' ability to communicate with the unit's assistant head nurse for the evening shift, who is also Filipina. The court observed that the rule is limited to the evening shift in one unit, and applies only to Tagalog. Because the rule was no more than a shift-specific directive tailored to respond to certain conflicts among identified staff nurses, the court found that the hospital did not intentionally discriminate on the basis of national origin. In a second suit, a federal appeals court rejected EEOC guidelines that treat workplace English-only rules as presumptively invalid. The court upheld an English-only rule in a plant that employs 33 workers, 24 of whom are Spanish-speaking.[126] The Civil Rights Act of 1964 "does not protect the ability of workers to express their cultural heritage at the workplace," the court declared. The introduction of such a policy does not have the same effect in every workplace, the court observed, and whether the policy creates a hostile work environment is a factual issue to be decided on a case-by-case basis. In a third case, the Seventh Circuit ruled that a hospital laboratory supervisor's remarks that an employee should "learn to speak English" cannot serve as the basis for a Title VII claim, unless the employee can show a link between the remarks and her cultural heritage.[127]

A federal trial court has ruled that a hospital's denial of medical staff privileges to a Palestinian-born surgical resident gave rise to a Title VII employment discrimination action.[128] The court acknowledged that the relationship between a hospital and the physicians it grants staff privileges to is an independent-contractor relationship rather than an employer–employee relationship. The court held, however, that the resident's prior employment by the hospital during his surgical residency qualifies him for Title VII protection. Once a contractual relationship of employment is established, Title VII governs the "terms, conditions, or privileges of employment," the court explained. The court found that the right to be considered for staff privileges at the hospital was clearly a fringe benefit of being a surgical resident, and that denial of these privileges would come under the protection of Title VII. The court dismissed the case, however, after concluding that the resident had not proved that the denial of privileges was due to his Palestinian origin.

Reverse Discrimination

As previously stated, Title VII of the Civil Rights Act of 1964 prohibits preferential hiring. Court challenges to voluntary affirmative action hiring or admission programs have been brought by members of nonminority groups, who have charged that they were denied jobs[129] or not admitted to an educational program[130] solely because they were members of a majority group. The U.S. Supreme Court considered the question of reverse discrimination in *Bakke v. Regents of the University of California.*[131] In *Bakke*, the Court held that it is unconstitutional for medical schools to maintain strict racial quotas where there has not been a finding of prior discrimination. Race, however, could be considered as a selection factor.

The touchstone of the law is whether all applicants are treated and evaluated equally. This does not mean that an employer cannot undertake a voluntary affirmative action program designed to remedy previous discrimination. The Supreme Court held in *Weber v. Kaiser Aluminum & Chemical Corp.*[132] that voluntary affirmative action programs that were based on "goals," instead of strict "quotas," would be upheld. In a 1987 California case, the Supreme Court ruled that a county did not violate Title VII by voluntarily adopting an affirmative action plan for hiring and promoting minorities and women.[133] The county plan was intended to increase the number of women and minorities in major job classifications in the transportation agency, where they traditionally had been underrepresented. Although the affirmative action plan did not set hiring quotas, it authorized the consideration of ethnicity or sex as a factor when evaluating qualified candidates for jobs in which members of these groups were poorly represented.

The Supreme Court approved the use of sex as one factor in determining which employee to promote. It noted that the plan was designed to remedy a conspicuous imbalance in the work force, and was a temporary measure intended to attain rather than maintain a balanced labor force. In addition, the affirmative action plan did not authorize blind hiring, but directed that numerous factors be taken into account in making hiring decisions. The Court found that the plan neither unnecessarily trammeled the rights of other employees, nor created an absolute bar to their advancement. The Supreme Court concluded that the decision to promote the female employee was made pursuant to an affirmative action plan that represents a moderate, flexible, case-by-case approach to gradually improving the representation of minorities and women.

Enforcement and Remedies under Title VII

Under Title VII, an individual who feels aggrieved may file a complaint with the EEOC. Members of the EEOC also have the power to initiate complaints.[134] The complaint need not contain the name of the individual on whose behalf the complaint is filed, as long as the Commission is informed as to the identity of that person.[135] This regulation is intended to protect the complainant from possible retaliation by employers or prospective employers.

Many states have enacted legislation similar to Title VII. In such states, the EEOC defers to the state fair employment practice (FEP) agency and allows the agency to attempt to resolve the dispute first.[136] As a result of the EEOC's deferral policy, a confusing set of procedural limitations has been imposed on complainants. If there is no state or local FEP agency to which the EEOC must defer, a complaint must be filed within 180 days of the alleged discriminatory act. If there is a state or local FEP agency, the complaint must be filed with the EEOC within 300 days of the alleged discrimination or within 30 days of final action by the state FEP agency, whichever is shorter.[137] Once a complaint is in the hands of a state or local FEP agency, the EEOC defers to that agency for 60 days. At the expiration of the 60 days, or whenever the FEP agency has completed its proceedings, whichever is shorter, the deferred charge is considered to be filed with the EEOC.[138] Under the Civil Rights Act of 1991, the time period for filing begins to run when the allegedly discriminatory system is adopted, when the employee falls within the system, or when the employee is injured by the system, whichever is most favorable to the employee.[139]

After a complaint is filed with the EEOC, the Commission notifies the employer within ten days and undertakes an investigation.[140] The employer may file a response with the agency.[141] The EEOC's investigatory powers are quite broad. The Commission may go beyond the specific allegations of the complaint and has the power to issue enforceable subpoenas.[142] After the initial investigation, the EEOC makes a determination as to whether there is reasonable cause to believe that an unlawful employment practice occurred. If reasonable cause is found, the Commission is required to try to resolve the issues by means of conciliation.[143] Conciliation efforts are confidential and may not be made public by the Commission or its employees.[144] If the conciliation effort succeeds, the employer and the EEOC sign a written agreement that sets forth the manner in which the employer agrees to remedy the situation.[145] A conciliation agreement has been ruled to have the same status as an enforceable contract.[146] If conciliation efforts fail, the EEOC may file suit against the employer. Prior to filing suit, the Commission must notify the employer in writing that conciliation efforts have been determined to be unsuccessful.[147]

If conciliation efforts fail, if the EEOC has failed to resolve a complaint within 180 days of filing, or if the Commission has found no reasonable cause to credit the allegations of the complaint, the complainant or others acting on his or her behalf may bring suit in federal court against the respondent. To file such a suit, however, the complainant must secure, in writing, a notice from the EEOC commissioner of the complainant's right to sue, known as a "right to sue letter."[148] In addition to an individual complainant's right to sue, the complainant may intervene in and join a suit brought by the EEOC or the attorney general against the employer. By the same token, the EEOC may intervene in and join a suit brought by an individual.[149] The Commission's failure to investigate and conciliate does not bar suit by a private complainant to whom it has granted the right to sue.[150]

The U.S. Code at 42 U.S.C. § 2000e-5(g) deals with remedies for individuals who allege unlawful employment discrimination under Title VII. It allows the court to order appropriate affirmative action, including reinstatement or hiring of employees with or without back pay for a period dating back to a maximum of two years before the complaint was filed with the EEOC. Such relief might include an order to hire a certain ratio of minority employees, for example. Although courts have used their broad injunctive powers extensively to remedy the impact of past discriminatory practices, hospitals should bear in mind that Title VII complaints against industry employers typically concern an individual complainant. In such cases, the courts have limited their relief to aiding the aggrieved individual.

Back pay awards are discretionary.[151] The Supreme Court, however, in *Albemarle Paper Co. v. Moody*,[152] has severely limited the discretion of lower courts in not awarding back pay. The court noted that the "central statutory purposes [of Title VII are aimed at] eradicating discrimination throughout the economy and making persons whole for injuries suffered through past discrimination."[153] The Court noted that any rule to limit the award of back pay would frustrate the statute's stated purpose of making individuals "whole." The Supreme Court has also ruled, however, that by making an unconditional offer of a previously denied position to a Title VII job bias claimant, an employer halts its potential back pay liability.[154] Back pay need not be awarded where the employer shows that the conduct in question was undertaken in good faith, reliance on, and in conformity with the written opinion of the EEOC.[155] A second limitation arises where the employer has been prejudiced by the complainant's conduct (e.g., where employees waited five years after the institution of their lawsuit before demanding back pay).[156]

The prevailing party in a Title VII case (other than the EEOC and the Attorney General) may be awarded attorneys' fees.[157] As with back pay, the failure of a trial judge to award attorneys' fees to a successful complainant has been held an abuse of the court's discretion because the fees are granted to encourage individuals to bring suit against employers who practice racial discrimination.[158] At one time, fee awards to prevailing employers were rare. The Supreme Court ruled in 1978 that a defendant employer or union that prevails in an action brought under Title VII may be awarded attorneys' fees if the court finds the action was frivolous, unreasonable, or without foundation.[159] More recently, the Third Circuit upheld a trial court's award of $10,000 in attorneys' fees to a non–health care employer who was sued by a former employee on a baseless Title VII discrimination claim.[160]

The Civil Rights Act of 1991 allows certain employees alleging discrimination in violation of Title VII to recover compensatory and punitive damages up to certain caps.[161] This statute resolves a split among federal courts concerning whether compensatory and punitive damages can be awarded in Title VII suits.[162]

A Title VII remedy may also take the form of a conciliation or settlement agreement, or a consent decree. Consent decrees, unlike settlement agreements, are subject to significant judicial review. A consent decree is an agreement between the parties that is submitted to the court to be entered in the form of a decree or an order. Violation of such a decree subjects the violator to the same penalties of contempt of court as are imposed for violation of a court order entered without the consent of the parties. Individuals who are a party to the suit have the option of joining or not joining in the consent decree. Those who choose not to join in the decree are entitled to initiate their own litigation, but, in so doing, these individuals must cover their own legal expenses. Those who choose to join in the consent decree are bound to accept its terms.

Recent Developments in Title VII Remedies

The split among circuits continues concerning whether individual supervisors can be liable for discrimination under Title VII. The Second Circuit has joined at least three other federal circuits in holding that an employer's "agent" cannot be held personally liable under Title VII.[163] Other circuits have held that supervisors can be liable for discrimination, however.[164]

In a health care case, a federal trial court in Missouri has ruled that individual supervisors cannot be personally liable for race discrimination under Title VII.[165] A hospital employee who was terminated sued two supervisors for discriminating against her on the basis of race in violation of Title VII. The supervisors asked the court to dismiss the claims against them, arguing that they could not be held individually liable under Title VII. The Missouri federal trial court noted that the Eighth Circuit had not yet addressed the issue, and noted that other circuits were split regarding whether supervisors can be liable under Title VII. Electing to follow the reasoning of the Ninth Circuit, the trial court ruled that individual supervisors cannot be held liable for race discrimination under Title VII and dismissed the claims against the supervisors in this case.

Defenses Available to the Employer

Title VII prohibits a wide variety of activities; however, it does contain several defenses to a charge of discrimination. A frequently used defense is the bona fide occupational qualification exception. To qualify for this exception, a hospital must be able to demonstrate that the factors upon which an employment decision is based are job-related and necessary for the successful handling of the job. If the employer can prove the existence of a reasonable BFOQ, the employer may consider those factors in employment-related decisions.[166]

Title VII allows an employer to advance employees based upon bona fide seniority and merit systems.[167] An employer may continue to use such systems even if they have an adverse effect on minority employees. The Supreme Court has held that Congress did not intend to upset existing seniority arrangements when it adopted Title VII in 1964, although the effect may be to grant Whites greater seniority than Blacks. In *International Brotherhood of Teamsters v. United States*,[168] the Court held that an otherwise neutral seniority system is not unlawful under Title VII solely because it perpetuates discrimination that preceded the Act. The decision of the Court comports with Title VII, which permits the maintenance of bona fide seniority and merit systems if they do not result from an intention to discriminate. In *American Tobacco Co. v. Patterson*, however, the Supreme Court ruled that the Title VII provision is not limited in application to seniority systems adopted before the effective date of the Act.[169] Emphasizing that seniority systems are afforded special treatment under Title VII, the Court concluded that it immunizes all bona fide seniority systems, and does not distinguish between the perpetuation of pre-Act and post-Act discriminatory impact.

An employer is free to use the results of professionally developed ability tests as a defense in its failure to hire or promote cases. The use of standardized ability tests is permissible if they are not used to discriminate. If these tests have an adverse impact on a protected group in statistical terms, however, the employer may be required to prove that such tests are both valid and job-related.[170] The EEOC has developed guidelines approved by the Supreme Court for showing that the tests are job-related.[171] The Civil Service Commission, the Department of Labor, and the Department of Justice jointly adopted the EEOC guidelines.[172]

An employer may also argue that the complaining employee did not file the lawsuit within the time period prescribed by the applicable statute of limitations. An employee, however, may obtain an extension by alleging a continuing violation (i.e., that the employer's discriminatory policies or practices are of a constantly recurring or continuing nature). The continuing violation doctrine applies only to acts or practices that are alleged to be discriminatory; it does not apply to the continuing effects of alleged past discriminatory acts. Further, the Civil Rights Act of 1991 establishes that the filing period for a Title VII challenge begins to run when the allegedly discriminatory system is adopted, when the employee falls within the system, or when the employee is injured by the system, whichever is most beneficial to the employee. [173]

Notice, Reporting, and Recordkeeping

Title VII requires all employers subject to its provisions to post certain notices and maintain certain employment records. Employers must post in conspicuous places notices provided by or approved by the EEOC that explain relevant sections of Title VII, including complaint-filing procedures. Failure to post required notices is punishable by a $100 fine for each offense.[174] Employers must also make reports and keep records in compliance with EEOC regulations or orders.[175] The EEOC requires employers with 100 or more employees to file an Employer Information Report EEO-1 annually, and to keep a copy of the most recent EEO-1 report available on its premises for inspection.[176] In addition, knowingly or willfully making false statements on an EEO-1 report is punishable by a fine of up to $10,000, a five-year jail term, or both.[177] The EEOC has the power to require additional or special reports.[178]

The EEOC requires employers to keep records on employee racial and ethnic identities. Although EEOC regulations do not require an employer to keep such records separate from employees' basic personnel information or records, the Commission strongly urges that employers do so.[179] Further, the EEOC requires that all employment and personnel records, including applications and records dealing with "hiring, promotion, demotion, transfer, lay-off or termination, rates of pay or other terms of compensation, and selection for training or apprenticeship," of all but temporary or seasonal employees be preserved for one year from the date of making or entering a record of personnel action.[180]

EQUAL PAY ACT OF 1963

The Equal Pay Act of 1963[181] was passed as an amendment to the Fair Labor Standards Act (FLSA) and, as such, is enforced in the same way as the FLSA. The law was designed to correct existing disparities in wages based solely on the sex of employees. The Equal Pay Act applies to every employer covered by the minimum wage law. In addition, although the Act is part of the FLSA, its coverage—which applies to state and local governments and their agencies and departments—is broader. With the exception of one unappealed decision,[182] the federal courts have concluded that the extension of the Equal Pay Act to state and local governments is constitutional.[183] The Equal Pay Act, unlike the FLSA, protects executive, administrative, and professional personnel.[184] The Act has a significant impact on hospitals due to the large numbers of female employees employed by such institutions. The Act requires that employees who perform equal work receive equal pay. Equal work is broadly defined as work that requires "equal skill, effort, and responsibility, and [that is] performed under similar working conditions."[185] The only exceptions recognized by the statute concern bona fide seniority systems, merit systems, or systems that measure earnings by the quantity or quality of production. The Act also recognizes that wages may be unequal as long as they are based upon a factor other than sex.[186]

What Is Equal Work?

Jobs are considered equal if they involve (1) equal skill, (2) equal effort, (3) equal responsibility, and (4) are performed under similar working conditions. If jobs are unequal with respect to any one of these four factors, then a wage differential may be justified. It must be noted, however, that "equal" does not mean "identical."

The courts, in a struggle to determine whether jobs are equal, have arrived at a practical definition of "equal work" as that which falls somewhere on a scale between identical work and similar or comparable work.[187] Regulations adopted by the EEOC state that the equal work standard does not require that comparable jobs be identical, only that they be substantially equal.[188] To determine whether two jobs are of an equal nature, the previously mentioned four factors must be measured on a similar scale.

Whether the equal pay standard does or does not apply depends upon an evaluation of "actual job requirements and performance."[189] The courts have ruled that each equal pay case must be decided on its own merits and cannot be applied on an industry-wide basis.[190] Thus, hospitals have been involved in innumerable cases on the issue of equal pay for nurse's aides and orderlies and equal pay for maids and porters. It is therefore not surprising that some courts in the aide-orderly cases have reached diametrically opposite conclusions on similar facts.

On the one hand, the determination of whether a job requires equal skill depends on an evaluation of "such factors as experience, training, education, and ability" and must be measured in terms of the performance requirements of the job.[191] On the other hand, equal effort "is concerned with the measurement of the physical or mental exertion needed for the performance of a job." Job factors that cause mental fatigue and stress, as well as those that alleviate fatigue, should be considered in determining the effort required by the job.[192] Coupled with a job's equal effort is the amount of responsibility assumed by the individual holding the particular position. "Responsibility is concerned with the degree of accountability required in the performance of the job, with the emphasis on the importance of the job obligation."[193] If the job responsibilities of the two similar positions are unequal, no discrimination will be found if the person who is paid less has fewer responsibilities.

The Equal Pay Act uses the term *similar working conditions* instead of the more exacting term *equal conditions.*[194] The use of the word *similar* implies that a flexible standard of similarity will be used as a basis for testing this requirement. For example, jobs in different departments are not necessarily performed under dissimilar working conditions.

In any lawsuit brought pursuant to the Equal Pay Act, the EEOC or the complainant must prove (1) the equality or substantial equality of work and (2) the existence of pay differentials between the male and female employees who perform the work. The employer must then prove that the criteria for distinguishing jobs and pay rates are based upon statutory exceptions or upon factors other than sex.

Hospital Employees

Hospitals have, in the past, been found in violation of the Equal Pay Act with respect to two groups of employees. At one time, litigation centered on the wage differential between aides and orderlies. Hospitals traditionally justified the payment of higher wages to male orderlies than to female nurse's aides by pointing to job duties unique to orderlies. Typically, a hospital would argue that, in addition to the duties performed by the female aides, the male orderlies

- catheterize male patients (female patients are catheterized by registered nurses [RNs] or licensed practical nurses [LPNs])
- set up traction
- perform male surgical skin preparations (female preparations done by LPNs or RNs) and other sterile techniques
- handle and install large oxygen tanks
- lift and transport patients
- subdue violent, combative, or confused patients
- work in the emergency department

Hospitals met with varied success in their attempts to prove that aides and orderlies do not have similar responsibilities and working conditions. Where hospitals were able to show that orderlies spent a substantial amount of their time doing most or all of the chores listed and that the aides did not do these chores, no equal pay violation was found.[195] If, however, aides were found to perform tasks similar to those performed by orderlies, such as catheterizations and preparation for surgery, differing pay scales for aides and orderlies have been held to violate the Equal Pay Act.[196] Likewise, courts found violations where the additional tasks performed by orderlies were only secondary or tertiary to the primary job of patient care that orderlies and aides shared and where the additional task occupied only a small percentage of the orderlies' time.[197]

Health care facilities should be alert to the potential for Equal Pay Act suits in other areas, also. Hospitals have not fared well in their efforts to prove that male custodian or porter jobs required greater skill, effort, or responsibility than female custodian or maid jobs.[198] Because job duties vary so widely, courts must apply the provisions of the Equal Pay Act on a case-by-case basis.[199]

In one case, a federal trial court held that a hospital had not violated the Equal Pay Act by compensating female nurse practitioners at a rate significantly lower than male physician assistants.[200] The court explained that its ruling did not concern the relative education, competence, or skills of nurse practitioners and physician assistants in general. In this case, however, although the jobs were substantially similar in terms of effort and working conditions, the physician assistant possessed greater skills, had more responsibility, and could legally perform a wider range of services than the nurse practitioners.

Comparable Worth

In the late 1970s, a new equal pay theory was tendered, largely as a result of the efforts of various women's rights groups. The theory, known as "comparable worth," states that jobs should be evaluated and rated, and that employees should be paid at a rate equal to their comparable worth to their employer. The theory is rooted in the rationale that whole classes of jobs, those traditionally held by women, are artificially undervalued and should be upgraded. Initially, the theory had no success in the courts.[201] In August 1980, however, the U.S. Court of Appeals for the Third Circuit in New Jersey ruled in a split decision that sex-based wage discrimination is prohibited under Title VII of the 1964 Civil Rights Act. The court emphasized that this applies even when jobs differ from one another and that Title VII extends beyond the limitations of the Equal Pay Act. A labor union had charged that, since 1939, an employer had paid women significantly less than men at its New Jersey plant, although the company's own job evaluations indicated that the same level of skill and responsibility was required of women as of men.[202]

In a 1985 case, however, the Ninth Circuit ruled that Washington State did not violate Title VII by adopting a compensation system that evaluated jobs according to the competitive market rather than comparable worth.[203]

Fringe Benefits

The EEOC has issued a regulation addressing the legality of fringe benefit plans that differentiate between male and female employees.[204] "Fringe benefits" include medical, hospital, accident, life insurance and retirement benefits, profit sharing and bonus plans, and leave. Under the regulation, the use of sex-based actuarial tables to calculate fringe benefits may not be justified under the "any other factor other than sex" exception to the Equal Pay Act. Further, employers may not defend on the ground that the cost of a fringe benefit is greater for one sex than for the other. Benefits conditioned on "head of household" or "principal wage earner" status will be closely scrutinized by the EEOC. Finally, employers that offer benefits to employees' spouses must do so for both sexes.

The U.S. Supreme Court has issued two important decisions regarding disparate retirement plans for male and female employees. In *City of Los Angeles v. Manhart*,[205] the Court rejected as unlawful an employer-paid pension system where premium rates for males and females were different, but annuity payments were equal. The higher premiums were based upon sex-based mortality tables. Specifically, the Court rejected the employer's argument that a differential in contributions exacted from men and women is lawful when based on a factor (longevity) other than sex.

In *Arizona Governing Committee v. Norris*,[206] the Supreme Court ruled that Arizona violated Title VII by offering female state employees lower monthly retirement benefits than male employees, although both groups contributed equal amounts. Using sex as a classification at the payout stage is prohibited, just as it is at the contribution stage under *Manhart*, the Court held. The differential monthly payments cannot be justified by the relative longevity of females, the Court ruled, as employees must be treated as individuals, not on the basis of characteristics of their class. Finally, the Court rejected the employer's argument that it was not liable because the payments were determined by outside insurers, finding that the employer was liable because it selected the insurers and contracted with them to provide the employees' retirement packages.

Defenses Available to the Employer

The primary defense to a charge that pay differentials between male and female employees violate the Equal Pay Act is to argue that the jobs in question require different levels of skill, effort, and responsibility, and are done under different working conditions. The second line of defense is to argue that pay differentials between the sexes are based upon the enumerated exceptions to the Equal Pay Act—a seniority system, a merit system, or a system based on quantity or quality of production—or that pay differentials are based upon factors other than sex.[207] Employers, however, have the burden of proving that their pay brackets fall within one of the exceptions listed or are based upon a factor other than sex; it must be shown that sex is not a factor in the determination of wage rates.

At one time, a Department of Labor regulation allowed wage differentials for employees enrolled in bona fide training programs.[208] The EEOC did not incorporate this exception to the Equal Pay Act in its regulations when it assumed enforcement of the Act, however. Employers conducting training programs should ensure that the program is open to both sexes, employees in the program know they are trainees, and the program follows a defined schedule.[209]

"Red circle rates" also may provide employers with a defense to allegations of Equal Pay Act violations.[210] The term "red circle rate" refers to a situation in which an employee with a long service record becomes unable to perform his or her job (due to ill health, for example) and is transferred to a lower paying position held by opposite-sex employees. Under these circumstances, the transferred employee may retain the previous, higher wage, because the wage differential is based on a factor other than sex.

Enforcement and Remedies

The Equal Pay Act is enforced by the EEOC. In response to conflicting court decisions concerning the validity of the transfer of power to enforce the Equal Pay Act from the Labor Department to the EEOC in 1979, Congress clarified in 29 *U.S.C.* Section 206 that the EEOC properly has enforcement power. The Equal Pay Act is enforced under the same procedures set forth in the FLSA. The Equal Pay Act does not allow an employer to remedy an equal pay violation by lowering the wages of any employee.[211] The maximum amount of civil damages for which an employer may be held liable is equal to the amount of the wage differential between male and female jobs, plus liquidated damages in an equal amount, and attorneys' fees.[212] The statute of limitations for recovering unpaid wages is two years, or three years for willful violations.[213]

Recent Development under the Equal Pay Act

The following case affects Equal Pay Act case law: A federal trial court in Florida dismissed a physician assistant's case against a hospital where the physician assistant claimed that the hospital paid him less for work that was equal or substantially similar to a group of predominantly female nurse practitioners.[214] The court found that the physician assistant did not establish a prima facie case under the Equal Pay Act because he did not identify a female nurse practitioner who received more pay for substantially equivalent work. Moreover, even if the physician assistant had identified a comparable nurse practitioner, the court agreed with the hospital's defense that the pay difference was due to factors other than sex. Specifically, the hospital asserted that the pay differential was justified by the differences in education and scope of practice between physician assistant and nurse practitioners and/or the fact that nurse practitioners were represented by a union whereas the physician assistants were not.

AGE DISCRIMINATION IN EMPLOYMENT ACT

Congress enacted the Age Discrimination in Employment Act,[215] commonly known as the ADEA, to "promote employment of older persons based on their ability rather than age; to prohibit arbitrary age discrimination in employment; [and] to help employers and workers find ways of meeting problems arising from the impact of age on employment."[216] The Act as originally enacted protected persons who are "at least 40 years of age, but less than 65 years of age."

In 1978, the Act was amended to broaden its coverage in the following respects: (1) the upper age limit on coverage was raised from 65 to 70, and (2) mandatory retirement, based on age, prior to age 70 was prohibited.[217] In 1986, Congress eliminated the upper age limit on coverage under the ADEA.[218] The law now protects workers above the age of 40 in matters such as hiring, compensation, job security, and other terms and conditions of employment.

The U.S. Court of Appeals for the Fifth Circuit has ruled that an employee cannot waive the right to file a discrimination charge with the EEOC because such a waiver is against public policy.[219] The court further ruled, however, and EEOC rules also state, that an employee can waive the right to bring a claim against the employer under the ADEA and waive the right to recover from the employer if the waiver is made knowingly and voluntarily.[220]

Prohibited Acts

The ADEA prohibits an employer of 20 or more persons engaged in an industry affecting commerce from discriminating against job applicants or employees over the age of 40 because of their age.[221] The Act was amended in 1974 to add federal, state, and local governments, and their agencies to the list of employers who must comply with the Act.[222] In 1983, the U.S. Supreme Court ruled that application of the ADEA to state and local governments is constitutionally valid because the ADEA does not unduly intrude upon state sovereignty.[223] Labor organizations and employment agencies are also subject to the provisions of the Act.[224]

The Act's language is quite similar to that of Title VII. It is unlawful for an employer

- to fail or refuse to hire or to discharge any individual or otherwise discriminate against any individual with respect to his compensation, terms, conditions, or privileges of employment because of such individual's age
- to limit, segregate, or classify his employees in any way that would deprive or tend to deprive any individual of employment opportunities or otherwise adversely affect his status as an employee because of such individual's age

- to reduce the wage rate of any employee in order to comply with this Act[225]

The ADEA prohibits discrimination against any employee or applicant who, in the past, has opposed practices made illegal by the ADEA or who has filed a charge, testified, or participated in any stage of an age discrimination case.[226] It is also unlawful for an employer to indicate "any preference, limitation, specification, or discrimination based on age" in notices or advertisements for employment.[227]

The ADEA prohibits discrimination by failing to hire or by discharging employees because of age. Therefore, it is unlawful to give preference to an employee or job applicant solely because the person is younger than 40. The Act does not forbid an employer to discriminate between two persons whose ages fall outside this range, for example, between two persons 25 and 35 years of age.

Employers may ask applicants to state their age or date of birth. Employers should be prepared, however, to justify such a request with a nondiscriminatory purpose, as the EEOC may closely scrutinize such a request.[228]

Discrimination in matters of compensation, terms, conditions, or privileges of employment is also prohibited. The term *compensation* includes all types and methods of remuneration paid to or on behalf of an employee for his or her employment.[229] Terms, conditions, and privileges of employment include, but are not limited to, job security, promotion, status, benefits (including overtime), leave (sick leave), vacation, holidays, career development programs, and seniority or merit systems that govern conditions such as transfer, assignment, job retention, layoff, and recall.

In 1989, the U.S. Supreme Court ruled that a disability retirement plan available only to disabled employees under age 60 and offering higher pensions than an age-and-service retirement plan was exempt from the ADEA as a bona fide benefit plan and not as a subterfuge to evade the purposes of the ADEA.[230] This controversial decision involved an Ohio state employee who retired at age 61 because of a medical disability and was required to accept a pension consisting of half of the amount of disability payments she would have received if she had retired before age 60. The employee charged the state with age discrimination. Both a trial court and an appeals court agreed that the disability plan was illegal as a subterfuge because the state had not shown any business or cost-related justification for excluding older employees.

The Supreme Court examined the meaning of "subterfuge." The employee argued that unless the cost of offering the benefit to older workers was shown to be higher, their exclusion was unjustified and therefore a subterfuge. Such cost-based justification is not required by the ADEA, the Court pointed out. To evade the purposes of the ADEA, a plan must be used to discriminate in a way forbidden by the ADEA, the Court reasoned. Because it found that bona fide employee benefit plans were exempt from coverage under the ADEA, the Court ruled that the subterfuge must be directed at discriminating in some other aspect of employment.

In response to the controversy surrounding the *Betts* decision, Congress adopted the Older Workers Benefit Protection Act of 1990 (OWBPA)[231] to amend the ADEA. Title I of OWBPA overturns the *Betts* ruling by adopting the equal benefit or equal cost rule. In general, an employer may not discriminate on the basis of age in employee benefits. If the cost of providing the same benefit is greater for older workers than for younger workers, however, the employer may offer a lesser benefit to the older workers, provided that the cost is the same as the benefit provided to younger workers. Some common benefit arrangements are allowed, however. These include early retirement incentive plans (as long as they are voluntary and consistent with the purposes of the ADEA), subsidized early retirement, and Social Security bridge payments. Title II of OWBPA also establishes minimum standards for the waiver of ADEA rights by employees and provides that such waivers are not valid unless they are "knowing" and "voluntary."[232]

The Supreme Court has recently returned to the issue of benefits under the ADEA. An employer does not violate the ADEA by interfering with an older employee's pension benefits that would have vested because of the number of years of service with the employer, the Supreme Court has ruled.[233] A 62-year-old employee was fired a few weeks before his pension benefits would have vested by virtue of his having worked for the company for ten years. Although both the trial court and the appeals court found the employer liable for age discrimination under the ADEA, the Supreme Court disagreed.

There is no disparate treatment under the ADEA when the factor motivating the employer is a factor other than the employee's age, the court held, finding years of service analytically different from age. The Court explained that a person under the age of 40 could have worked for a company for more than ten years, and an older employee could be a new hire. Therefore, the court reasoned, a decision based on years of service is not necessarily age based. The Court pointed out, however, that the employer may violate the ADEA if the employer assumes a correlation between age and pension status and acts on that assumption. Further, there may be dual liability under the Employee Retirement Income Security Act (ERISA) and the ADEA when the decision to fire an employee about to vest in pension benefits is a result of age rather than years of service.

Exceptions and Exemptions

The U.S. Code at 29 U.S.C. §623(f) lists the exceptions that justify distinctions based on age.

Bona Fide Occupational Qualification

The language of the BFOQ exception in the ADEA is similar to that in Title VII.[234] Like the Title VII exception, the BFOQ exception to the ADEA has been narrowly construed and determined on a case-by-case basis; the burden of establishing age as a BFOQ is on the employer. One commonly accepted BFOQ is that which is imposed by law or regulation for the safety and convenience of the public.

Reasonable Factors Other Than Age

Under the ADEA, employers may differentiate among employees based on reasonable factors other than age.[235] A reasonable factor other than age may be a physical fitness requirement if it is necessary to the performance of a specific job.

Bona Fide Seniority Systems

As long as it is not a subterfuge to evade the Act, a bona fide seniority system may be used by an employer.[236] To qualify, a seniority system must be based primarily on length of service, although factors such as merit, capacity, or ability may be recognized by an employer. A valid seniority system gives greater benefits and rights to those employees with longer service; however, a system that merely perpetuates pre-Act discrimination is not bona fide.

Employee Benefit Plans and Mandatory Retirement Ages

Under the ADEA, an employer may not require employees to retire solely because of age.[237] There is an exception for bona fide executives who are entitled to retire with a pension of at least $44,000 yearly.[238]

Exemptions

Pursuant to its power to establish reasonable exemptions in the ADEA, the EEOC has exempted certain apprenticeship programs.[239]

Courts are divided on the issue of whether the ADEA applies to hospitals affiliated with a particular religion or church. In one case, a hospital chaplain who was discharged sued the church-affiliated hospital under the ADEA.[240] The Eighth Circuit ruled in favor of the hospital, holding that to apply the age discrimination statute to the chaplain's discharge would constitute unconstitutional government interference with religion. In a second case, however, a federal trial court in Pennsylvania allowed a terminated employee to bring an ADEA suit against a church-affiliated hospital, reasoning that the facility was not exempt from the federal statute because identifying the reason for the employee's discharge does not require an examination of the validity of church doctrine.[241]

Enforcement and Remedies

The ADEA is enforced by the EEOC, in accordance with the powers, remedies, and procedures of the FLSA.[242]

Although the remedies afforded complainants under the ADEA and FLSA are similar, there are significant differences between the two laws. Under the ADEA, liquidated damages, an amount equal to the back pay due after violation of the Act has been established, may be granted only where it is shown that an employer's violation was willful.[243] The U.S. Supreme Court has clarified and reaffirmed the standard for liquidated damages.[244] The Court recognized that there has been widespread confusion about the standard, with some courts incorrectly believing that an employer who knowingly relies on age in reaching a decision invariably commits a knowing or reckless violation of the ADEA. If an employer incorrectly but in good faith and nonrecklessly believes that the law allows a particular age-based decision, liquidated damages should not be imposed, the Court explained. The Court clarified another point of confusion by ruling that once a willful violation has been shown, the employee is not required to show that the employer's conduct was outrageous, provide direct evidence of the employer's motivation, or prove that age was the predominant rather than a determinative factor in the employment decision. Finally, the Court ruled that the standard for liquidated damages not only applies when the violation is a formal, facially discriminatory policy, but also when it is an informal decision by the employer that was motivated by the employee's age.

The ADEA requires the EEOC, before suit, to attempt to affect voluntary compliance with the Act through informal conciliation, conferences, and persuasion.[245] The statute of limitations may be tolled for a period of up to one year while the EEOC attempts to affect voluntary compliance with the requirements of the Act.[246]

The ADEA requires an individual, who is initiating an action, to file a notice of intent to sue with the EEOC within 180 days of the alleged discrimination and at least 60 days before suit is commenced.[247] Strict compliance with the 180-day notice requirement of the ADEA is not always necessary.[248] An aggrieved individual may file a private lawsuit 60 days after filing administrative charges.[249] Individuals must, however, sue within two years of the alleged discriminatory action or within three years of alleged willful violations.[250]

When a state has an age discrimination law similar to the federal Act, the ADEA requires an individual to file his or her complaint first with the state and wait 60 days (or fewer if the state action is terminated before the expiration of 60 days) before seeking federal relief.[251] When an individual has filed a complaint with the state, the Act extends the time for filing of intent to sue to 300 days after the alleged discriminatory action has taken place.[252]

If the employer prevails in an age discrimination case, the EEOC may be ordered to pay the employer's fees and expenses, according the Fourth Circuit.[253] The court relied on the Equal Access to Justice Act, which provides that a court shall award such expenses to the prevailing party unless the court finds that the government's position was substantially justified. The ADEA authorizes a jury trial of any issue of fact in an action brought under the ADEA.[254]

Recordkeeping Requirements

All nongovernmental employers subject to the ADEA must maintain for three years those payroll or other records for each employee that contain (1) name, (2) address, (3) date of birth, (4) occupation, (5) rate of pay, and (6) weekly earnings. All health care employers subject to the Act must keep for one year personnel records relating to the following:

- job applications, resumes, or any other form of inquiry when submitted in response to the employer's notice of job opening, including records relating to the failure or refusal to hire any person
- promotion, demotion, transfer, selection for training, recall, or discharge of any employee
- job orders submitted to unemployment agencies or labor organizations for labor recruitment purposes
- test papers that indicate the results of employment tests
- results of physical examinations considered in connection with any personnel action

- any advertisements or notices to the public or employees concerning job openings, promotions, training programs, or opportunities for overtime work
- benefit plans and seniority and merit systems for at least one full year after termination of the plans[255]

Recent Developments under the Age Discrimination in Employment Act

An individual suing a former employer under the ADEA can recover for illegal age discrimination even if the individual was replaced with another employee over age 40, the U.S. Supreme Court has ruled.[256] Employees suing under the ADEA may base a claim on the same hostile environment analysis long recognized under Title VII, the Sixth Circuit has ruled in a case of first impression.[257] A hospital billing clerk sued her employer under the ADEA, arguing that her supervisor created a hostile working environment for older workers by making remarks such as, "I don't think women over 55 should be working," and "old people should be seen and not heard." Noting that no federal appeals court has addressed the issue, the Sixth Circuit determined that a hostile working environment can trigger an ADEA discrimination claim if the employee shows that he or she was harassed because of age and that the harassment created an objectively intimidating, hostile, or offensive work environment. In this case, the supervisor's comments, although age-based and rude, were not sufficiently severe or humiliating to serve as the basis for recovery. Thus, the court ruled in favor of the hospital.

THE REHABILITATION ACT OF 1973

In 1973, Congress enacted the Vocational Rehabilitation Act, extending employment-related protections to employees and applicants for employment with disabilities.[258] A major source of confusion about the Act concerns two critical sections, Sections 503[259] and 504,[260] that apply to different parties. Section 503 applies to government contractors with contracts exceeding $10,000 in value. Section 504 applies to employers who are recipients of federal financial assistance. Of the two sections, Section 504 is the most generally applicable to health care institutions.

Section 504 provides:

> No otherwise qualified individual with a disability in the United States . . . shall, solely by reason of her or his disability, be excluded from the participation in, be denied the benefits of, or be subjected to discrimination under any program or activity receiving Federal financial assistance. . . .[261]

Initially, it was not clear whether Section 504 of the Rehabilitation Act applied to hospitals, although courts generally held that Medicare and Medicaid payments constitute federal financial assistance, making hospitals receiving such funds covered by the Act.[262] In 1988, Congress resolved any doubt by amending the Rehabilitation Act to specifically cover health care organizations that receive federal financial assistance.[263]

Courts have applied Section 504 to protect employees of institutions that receive federal financial assistance, as well as to the persons who are beneficiaries of federally financed programs. Recently, federal courts have allowed hospital employees, as well as patients, to bring Section 504 discrimination suits.[264]

In 1987, Congress broadened the application of Section 504 by enacting the Civil Rights Restoration Act, which states that the recipients of federal funds must comply with civil rights laws throughout their operations, not just in the specific program or activity receiving the funds.[265]

Defining Disability

The first step in determining whether an individual is within the protection of the Rehabilitation Act is assessing whether the complaining individual has a disability. Although the Vocational Rehabilitation Act and its amended regulations address the issue, identifying who is within the definition remains difficult. The regulations interpreting the Act indicate that the term *disability* should be defined broadly.[266] The statute divides the definition into three parts:

> [I]ndividual with a disability means any person who (i) has a physical or mental impairment which substantially limits one or more of such person's major life activities, (ii) has a record of such an impairment, or (iii) is regarded as having such an impairment.[267]

The regulations further define each of these statutory categories. For example, "physical or mental impairment" specifically includes cosmetic disfigurement, mental illness or retardation, and learning disabilities.[268] One may have a record of an impairment even if it is based on a misdiagnosis.[269] Further, a person's handicap may result solely from the attitudes and perceptions of others.[270]

A morbidly obese job applicant is protected by the Rehabilitation Act, a federal appeals court has ruled.[271] The applicant, who was 5' 2" and weighed more than 320 pounds, had worked as an institutional attendant at a state residential facility for mentally retarded persons before and left voluntarily with a "spotless" record. Although the applicant passed the required physical, the facility refused to reemploy her, claiming that she was not capable of evacuating patients in an emergency, was likely to be absent frequently, and was apt to file workers' compensation claims because her obesity would lead to poor health. The First Circuit upheld a $100,000 jury verdict in favor of the applicant, upholding the jury's finding that the facility discriminated against the applicant on the basis of a disability. The Rehabilitation Act prohibits discrimination based on perceived disabilities, as well as actual disabilities, the court noted. The applicant presented sufficient evidence to the jury to find either that she was actually disabled as a result of morbid obesity, or that the facility perceived that she was; thus triggering the Rehabilitation Act's prohibition on discriminatory hiring. The court concluded that as a person with a disability otherwise qualified for the institutional assistant position, the applicant was entitled to the jury's verdict.

Who Is Otherwise Qualified?

The second step in determining whether an individual is protected by the Act is assessing whether the individual is "otherwise qualified" for the benefit or employment, as the Rehabilitation Act prohibits discrimination only against otherwise qualified individuals with disabilities. The definition of *otherwise qualified* is closely intertwined with the concept of reasonable accommodation. Specifically, an otherwise qualified person with a disability is one who, "with reasonable accommodation, can perform the essential functions of the job in question."[272] For example, a Veterans Administration hospital did not discriminate against a housekeeping aide with arthritis, whom it discharged due to excessive absences because the aide was not otherwise qualified for the position, a federal appeals court held.[273] The aide was not otherwise qualified for the position because regular attendance was an essential function of the job. Acknowledging that employers must make reasonable accommodations, including schedule modifications, for handicapped employees, the court ruled that the hospital could not accommodate the aide's unpredictable absences without undue hardship, thus excusing the employer from accommodation. Because the hospital had no duty to accommodate the aide, he could not meet the position's requirements and was not otherwise qualified for the position. Thus, the court held, the aide was not protected by the Rehabilitation Act.

Similarly, a head nurse who consistently reported late to work due to her mental illness was not protected by the Rehabilitation Act, the Second Circuit has ruled, because she was not "otherwise qualified" to fulfill the requirements of the head nurse position.[274] The head nurse, on medication to treat her severe depression, usually arrived for her 8:00 A.M. shift after 10:00 A.M. After being counseled about her tardiness, she requested that her hours be changed to 10:00 A.M.–6:30 P.M., stating that she needed to work a later shift because she was under a physician's care for extreme stress. After her request for a change of work schedule was denied, she filed a complaint with the EEOC and subsequently sued. The Second Circuit ruled that because the nurse's illness and medication regimen interfered with her ability to arrive at work on time, she was a handicapped person. The court also found, however, that she was not otherwise qualified to do the job. A qualified handicapped person, the court explained, is one who with or without reasonable accommodation can perform the essential functions of the job. In this case, the earlier shift was a critical requirement of the position of head nurse because the head nurse is the only management person on the unit during the shift. In addition, the head nurse must consult with the night supervisor as to patient treatment modifications, and must attend several early morning meetings. The court therefore concluded that the hospital had not violated the Rehabilitation Act.[275]

Drugs and Alcohol

Hospitals assessing the potential for liability for discharging an illegal drug user or alcoholic must determine the current status of the employee. Current alcoholics and drug addicts are specifically excluded from the definitions of "individual with a disability,"[276] whereas those who have recovered from their impairments are covered. Current users of illegal drugs are also excluded. Because only otherwise qualified persons with disabilities are protected by the law, a hospital could argue that a job applicant is not otherwise qualified for employment because prior drug addiction or alcoholism would prevent the individual from performing the duties of a job or would constitute a direct threat to the safety of others. This argument is only likely to be successful if the addiction occurred recently.

Contagious Diseases

Persons with contagious diseases are handicapped persons entitled to protection against discrimination under Section 504 of the Rehabilitation Act, the U.S. Supreme Court has ruled.[277] The case involved an elementary school teacher who was discharged after suffering a third relapse of tuberculosis within two years. The teacher sued the school board, alleging that her dismissal constituted discrimination on the basis of handicap. A federal trial court ruled that Congress did not intend persons with contagious diseases to be included within the definition of handicapped persons under the Act.

The U.S. Supreme Court ruled, however, that a person with a record of physical impairment is not excluded from coverage under the Act simply because the person is contagious. Although the definition of handicapped is broad, the Court explained, only those who are both handicapped and otherwise qualified for the job are eligible for relief. In determining if a person with a contagious disease is otherwise qualified, the Court ruled, several facts, based on reasonable medical judgments, must be elicited. Such facts include the nature, duration, and severity of the risk, and the probability that the disease will be transmitted and cause varying degrees of harm. The final step is to determine whether the employer could reasonably accommodate the employee.

A person who was excluded from a federally funded hospital's drug and alcohol treatment program because he tested positive for HIV, although he was asymptomatic, was handicapped within the meaning of the Rehabilitation Act, a federal district court in California ruled.[278] The hospital contended that its policy of excluding seropositive people from the program was to protect other patients and that contagiousness alone was not a handicap. The court ruled, however, that discrimination based on fear of contagion was clearly discrimination based on handicap.

A nurse who refused to divulge the results of his HIV test did not meet the definition of handicapped under Section 504, a federal trial court held, ruling that the hospital who discharged the nurse had not discriminated against him.[279] The nurse had argued that he was handicapped because the hospital perceived him as HIV positive and Section 504 defines handicapped persons to include those regarded as impaired. The trial court ruled, however, that the hospital fired the nurse because he refused to comply with its infection control policy and not because it perceived him as HIV positive. An appeals court upheld this ruling, finding that the nurse had failed to establish that the hospital's sole reason for terminating him was the possibility that he was infected.[280]

Recent Developments in Defining Disability

The following recent cases illustrate the difficulty of determining who is covered by the Rehabilitation Act.

- A physician rejected from admission to a hospital's residency program cannot recover for disability discrimination under either the Americans with Disabilities Act (ADA) or the Rehabilitation Act because his physical impairment, an eye condition known as strabismus, was not a disability under the antidiscrimination statutes, the Seventh Circuit has ruled.[281] Strabismus causes eye strain and fatigue faster in people who suffer from it than in people with normal eyesight. The federal appeals court refused to order the hospital to admit the physician to its residency program because strabismus did not significantly impact the physician's major life activities. The physician did not prove that he was substantially limited in his career because he did not submit evidence showing that all residency programs require long shifts. Further, the physician's ophthalmologist did not state whether the physician could perform the 36-hour shift required for the hospital's residency program while suffering from strabismus. Finally, the appeals court found that the trial court properly doubted the physician's statements with regard to the severity of his eye condition, because the physician's work history showed that he had the ability to work long hours under demanding circumstances.

- An operating room technician who tested false positive for HIV does not qualify for protection under the Rehabilitation Act according to a federal trial court in Pennsylvania.[282] After being stuck by a needle while assisting in surgery, a surgical technician tested HIV positive. As a result of the positive test result, the hospital placed the technician on a paid leave of absence. After two follow-up tests at a second facility showed that the technician was in fact HIV negative, she returned to work. After suffering a second accidental cut in the operating room, the technician sought an indefinite leave of absence to determine whether she wished to continue working in the health care field. She later sued, claiming that the hospital discriminated against her on the basis of disability in violation of the Rehabilitation Act. The court ruled in favor of the hospital, finding that the Rehabilitation Act did not cover the technician. First, because the technician claimed she was disabled because the hospital regarded her as HIV positive, the court examined the hospital's decision to place her on a leave of absence in light of her supposed HIV-positive status. Because she would have posed a direct threat to surgical patients, the court ruled, she was not otherwise qualified for the position, and therefore was not within the Act's protection. Second, the court rejected the nurse's claim that fear of HIV infection constitutes a protected disability such that the hospital should have granted her an indefinite leave of absence. The technician did not show that her fear was a mental disorder covered by the Act, the court found. Further, fear of HIV infection does not qualify as a disability because inability to perform a particular job is not a substantial limitation of a major life activity, the court reasoned. Thus, the court concluded, the technician cannot recover under the Act.

- A New York federal trial court properly instructed a jury that it could consider off-duty conduct when determining whether a hospital employee came within the protection of the Rehabilitation Act, the Second Circuit has ruled.[283]
- A hospital that discharged an HIV-positive operating room technician did not violate the ADA or the Rehabilitation Act, a federal district court in Michigan has ruled.[284] Hospital officials developed a belief that a technician was infected with HIV and requested that he submit to an HIV test. When the technician refused to submit to testing, or to accept an alternative position in a nonpatient care unit of the hospital, he was laid off. The technician, as a matter of law, has a contagious disease that poses a direct threat to the health and safety of patients undergoing surgical procedures, the court held. Acknowledging that the risk of HIV transmission from surgical technician to patient is remote, the court reasoned that transmission invariably has fatal consequences, and therefore the threat to patient safety posed by the technician performing his duties in the operating room is significant. Moreover, the hospital did all that was required to accommodate the technician by offering him a position that would have allowed him to

avoid direct patient contact. Because the technician posed a significant risk to others that cannot be eliminated by reasonable accommodation, he is not "otherwise qualified" to perform his job, and thus his discharge does not constitute unlawful discrimination under the ADA or the Rehabilitation Act, the court ruled.

Employment Practices under Section 504

Section 504 prohibits employment discrimination against a qualified handicapped employee solely because of a handicap. A hospital must make all employment decisions without regard to the physical or mental handicaps of otherwise qualified employees.[285] The regulations also prohibit an employer from participating in any contractual or other relationship that has the effect of subjecting qualified handicapped applicants or other employees to discrimination. Section 504 specifically applies to the following:

- recruitment, advertising, and the processing of applications
- hiring, upgrading, promotion, award of tenure, demotion, transfer, layoff, termination, right of return from layoff, and rehiring
- rates of pay or any other form of compensation and changes in compensation
- job assignments, job classifications, organizational structures, position descriptions, lines of progression, and seniority lists
- leaves of absence, sick leave, or any other leave
- fringe benefits available by virtue of employment, whether or not administered by recipients
- selection for financial support for training, including apprenticeships, professional meetings, conferences, and other related activities, and selection for leaves of absence to pursue training
- employer-sponsored activities, including social or recreational programs
- any terms, conditions, or privileges of employment[286]

Recent Developments in Employment Practices

Under certain circumstances, failure to accommodate a protected employee may be construed as termination of employment. A nurse working at a Veteran's Administration (VA) outpatient clinic may sue her employer for constructive discharge under the Rehabilitation Act based on allegations that the clinic refused to make reasonable accommodations for her hearing disability, a federal district court in Massachusetts has ruled. The nurse alleged that her hearing condition worsened over a two-year period during which time her employer rejected her repeated requests for transfer to a nonpatient unit. Moreover, the employer never provided the nurse with medical equipment, including a stethoscope for the hearing impaired, to accommodate her disability. Although an employer's refusal to provide reasonable accommodation to a disabled employee usually does not amount to constructive discharge, the court declared, in this case additional factors may justify such a claim. The court highlighted the nurse's allegations that her supervisors and coworkers demeaned her and told her that she was incompetent because of her disability. Under those circumstances, the case should proceed to trial to determine whether the nurse was subjected to a working environment so hostile that a reasonable person in her position would have resigned, the court held.[287]

Reasonable Accommodation

The definition of reasonable accommodation has been subject to continuing controversy. Section 504 deals only with discrimination against qualified handicapped persons. The regulations define a qualified handicapped person as one who, "with reasonable accommodation, can perform the essential functions of the job in question."[288] Therefore, a hospital may not insist that a handicapped employee perform all aspects or functions of the job, but only those that are "essential."

The courts have provided few examples of what constitutes "reasonable accommodation." Accommodation could be achieved by a health care employer if the employer modified work schedules, restructured jobs, and embarked on physical modifications or relocations of particular offices or jobs. The regulations recognize that "undue hardship" might be related to the cost of making the accommodations.[289] Factors to be considered in determining whether an accommodation constitutes an undue hardship include the size of the employer, nature of the work force, and cost of the accommodation.[290]

The supreme court of West Virginia has provided an illustration of what "reasonable accommodation" could mean in a hospital setting.[291] A hospital custodian was unable to perform heavy lifting or prolonged bending activities after sustaining a back injury. The court ruled that the hospital's decision to terminate the custodian because it could not find a position she was able to fill did not constitute a failure to reasonably accommodate her. "Reasonable accommodation" may demand restructuring a job to make it accessible to an employee, the court concluded, but does not extend to creating a new job tailored to the capabilities of the employee or transferring the employee to a job for which he or she was not hired.

The U.S. Supreme Court has reviewed Section 504 in several cases. In *Southeastern Community College v. Davis*,[292] for example, the Court made a narrow interpretation of the statutory phrase "otherwise qualified handicapped individual." The Court found that a community college covered by Section 504 was not required to admit a deaf individual to a registered nurse training program. The Court held that "an otherwise qualified person is one who is able to meet all of a program's requirements in spite of his handicap." The Court stated that physical qualifications may be considered as part of a program's requirements in a proper situation.

The Court further indicated that Section 504 does not require an employer to take affirmative action with respect to handicapped applicants. The language of the Court's decision implied that an employer could not be required to make extensive modifications of existing programs to accommodate a handicapped applicant. The Court cautioned that there is a fine line between optional extensive modifications and required reasonable accommodations.

A hospital did not violate the Rehabilitation Act when it transferred a surgical technician to a clerical position in the purchasing department after the technician revealed that he was HIV positive in a newspaper article, a federal appeals court has held.[293] The technician disclosed in a newspaper article that he was HIV positive and worked as a surgical assistant, naming the facility at which he worked. The hospital then reassigned him to the purchasing department as a procurement assistant. The technician sued the hospital for discrimination on the basis of disability under Section 504, arguing that he should have been transferred to a position involving patient contact. The court upheld the transfer, ruling that the hospital had no duty to offer reasonable accommodation because the only accommodation that would reduce the risk of HIV transmission to patients would be to eliminate an "essential function" of the job—presence in the operating room. Further, the court rejected the technician's argument that the hospital should have transferred him to a position involving patient contact. When reasonable accommodation is impossible, the employer may transfer the employee to any position as long as it does not deprive the employee of any reasonably available opportunities.

On the other hand, unnecessarily restricting an employee's duties on the basis of a disability may constitute discrimination. Because there is no meaningful likelihood that an HIV-positive pharmacist can transmit the acquired immune deficiency syndrome (AIDS)–causing virus to others, a hospital violated the Rehabilitation Act by offering to hire the pharmacist but restricting his duties, an administrative law judge (ALJ) has ruled.[294] The hospital made a job offer to a pharmacist, but withdrew the offer after a preemployment physical revealed that he was infected with HIV. When the pharmacist filed a complaint with the Department of Health and Human Services (HHS), the hospital reoffered him the position, but barred him from preparing intravenous materials. The ALJ dismissed the hospital's contention that the restriction was necessary to prevent transmission of HIV, stating that it was based on mere speculation and that the performance of the full range of duties would not pose a significant risk for other employees or patients.

Application and Interview Questions

Section 504's regulations prohibit any inquiry on an employment application or in an employment interview about an applicant's handicaps. The regulations, however, do permit a hospital to ask whether the applicant is able to perform the job in question.[295] The prohibition against inquiry into possible handicaps makes the applicant the judge of his or her competence to perform the job.

The regulations also prohibit "any employment tests or other selection criterion that screens out . . ." handicapped persons unless the tests are shown to be job related and nondiscriminatory alternatives are not available.[296] Further, the regulations provide that an employer may not subject handicapped employment applicants to physical examinations unless all applicants for the job are required to take the same physical examination.[297]

The regulations also limit how the results of such examinations may be used. In general, all information obtained during the course of physical examinations must be treated as confidential medical records. There are only three exceptions to this duty of confidentiality.

1. Supervisors and managers may be informed of restrictions on the work or duties of handicapped persons and of the necessary accommodation.
2. First-aid and safety personnel may be informed, where appropriate, if the condition might require emergency treatment.
3. Government officials investigating compliance with the law must be provided relevant information.[298]

Although an employer is prohibited from discriminating against qualified handicapped persons solely because of their handicap, a hospital may refuse to hire an applicant who is not qualified for a position due to the behavioral manifestations of the handicap.

> [An employer] may hold a drug addict or alcoholic to
> the same standard of performance and behavior
> to which it holds others. . . . In other words, while an

alcoholic or drug addict may not be denied services or be disqualified from employment solely because of his or her condition, the behavioral manifestations of the condition may be taken into account in determining whether he or she is qualified.[299]

Therefore, an employer may refuse to hire an alcoholic who has had a record of excessive absenteeism, although the absenteeism was the result of the employee's alcoholism.

Notice, Reporting, and Recordkeeping

All institutions receiving financial assistance from HHS are required to file assurances of compliance forms.[300] The assurance usually obligates the recipient only for the period of time that assistance is received. Filing the form in no way limits the institution's right to challenge in federal court the legality of any part of the regulations.

Hospitals receiving federal financial assistance are required to conduct a self-evaluation,[301] during which they review all practices and the effects of such practices on handicapped individuals. Each institution is also required to consult with interested parties, including handicapped persons; after such consultation, the hospital must modify any policies or practices that do not meet the requirements of the regulations. The hospital is required to keep a written account of the evaluation. This record must include

- a list of the interested persons consulted
- a description of the areas examined and any problems identified
- a description of any modifications made and of any remedial steps taken

This written self-evaluation must be retained for a period of three years and be made available for public inspection.[302]

Each employer must designate someone to coordinate compliance efforts. Hospitals are also required to adopt a grievance procedure to handle complaints alleging violations of the regulation; however, this procedure need not apply to applicants who are not hired.[303]

The regulations require a hospital to take appropriate steps to notify applicants, beneficiaries, and employees that it does not discriminate on the basis of an individual's handicap. No specific methods of notification are required; they may include "the posting of notices, publication in newspapers and magazines, placement of notices in [the employer's] publication, and distribution of memorandum or other written communications."[304]

Section 504's regulations specify that, as a federal statute, it supersedes any contrary state or local law. Employers facing possible inconsistent state or local laws should seek professional counsel.[305]

Enforcement and Remedies

Because Section 504 of the Rehabilitation Act is substantively similar to Title I of the ADA, which also prohibits employment discrimination on the basis of disability, enforcement of these two statutes are intertwined. The EEOC and the Department of Justice have issued joint regulations outlining the enforcement procedures for complaints that fall within the overlapping jurisdiction of Section 504 of the Rehabilitation Act and Title I of the ADA.[306] According to background information issued with the regulation, each federal agency that provides funds to private employers (hereinafter, a Section 504 agency) is responsible for enforcing the Rehabilitation Act with respect to the funded programs. At the same time, the EEOC is responsible for implementing Title I of the ADA.[307] Because complaints of disability discrimination may contain claims under both statutes, the final regulations require a Section 504 agency that receives a complaint to refer the complaint to the EEOC whenever the complaint solely alleges discrimination against a single individual.[308] The exceptions to this rule are cases where the EEOC specifically lacks jurisdiction, or where the employee specifically requests that the relevant Section 504 agency retain jurisdiction. Further, Section 504 agencies will process any complaints that allege a pattern or practice of discrimination in employment, or allege discrimination both in employment and in other services or practices covered by Section 504.[309]

Complaints will be investigated either by the Section 504 agency or the EEOC, depending on where the complaint was filed and if it was referred. If the complaint was investigated by the EEOC, the EEOC may issue a "right to sue" letter to the complaining employee, enter into a settlement with the employer, or undertake enforcement action.[310] If the complaint was referred by a Section 504 agency, the EEOC notifies the agency of the result and provides the agency with an opportunity to determine whether further action is necessary.[311] In the case of a violation, the Section 504 agency may withdraw its financial assistance.[312]

Recent Developments in Remedies

A hospital employee who claimed she was discharged because of her learning disabilities and speech impediment after 12 years of employment in the laundry department can seek compensatory and punitive damages as well as a jury trial under the Rehabilitation Act, according to a federal district court in Pennsylvania.[313] Other circuit courts have held that compensatory damages are available under the Rehabilitation Act.[314] Also, one circuit court has held that, when requested by the plaintiff, a jury trial is constitutionally required under the Rehabilitation Act.[315] The court reasoned that the discharged employee's request for back pay constitutes a request for compensatory damages that triggers the jury-trial right.

AMERICANS WITH DISABILITIES ACT OF 1990

The ADA, representing a landmark in civil rights legislation, became law on July 26, 1990.[316] The ADA prohibits discrimination against individuals with disabilities in private employment, public services and transportation, public accommodations, and telecommunications services. The ADA follows the same principles as the Rehabilitation Act. Health care institutions seeking judicial interpretation of this relatively new law may look to opinions addressing the Rehabilitation Act for guidance.

The term "disability" is broadly defined and includes any individual who has a physical or mental impairment that substantially limits one or more major life activities, who has a record of such impairment, or who is regarded as having such an impairment.[317] The EEOC regulations also specifically protect persons who have AIDS or HIV, as well as persons who are undergoing rehabilitation for substance abuse.[318] Current users of illegal drugs are not protected, however, and employers are free to test applicants for illegal drug use.[319]

Title I of the ADA specifically prohibits an employer from discriminating against a qualified individual with a disability in job application procedures, hiring, discharge, compensation, training, and any other conditions and privileges of employment.[320] The law covers all employers with 15 or more full-time employees.[321] An employer may not use standards or methods of selection that have the effect of discriminating on the basis of disability unless the standards or tests are directly job related and are consistent with business necessity.[322] In addition, an employer must reasonably accommodate disabled individuals who are otherwise qualified to do a job, unless making reasonable accommodations would impose an undue hardship on the employer.[323] An employer will be liable for discrimination by denying job opportunities to a qualified individual with a disability if the denial is based on the need to make reasonable accommodation. Examples of "reasonable accommodation" in the ADA include making existing facilities readily accessible to disabled individuals, job restructuring, providing qualified readers or interpreters, and purchasing or modifying equipment.[324]

Defining Disability

The EEOC has issued a compliance guide for the agency's use in designating disabilities covered under the ADA.[325] The guide clarifies the ADA's definition of "disability," by explaining the terms within that definition as interpreted by court decisions and earlier EEOC materials. Of particular significance, the guidelines represent the first federal document to state that individuals with a genetic predisposition to develop illness, disease, or other disorders are protected under the ADA. The compliance manual offers the example of an employee whose genetic profile reveals an increased susceptibility to colon cancer. Although the employee is asymptomatic and may never develop colon cancer, the prospective employer who withdraws a job offer because of concerns about productivity, insurance costs, and attendance violates the ADA by treating the employee as having an impairment that substantially limits a major life activity. According to the manual, EEOC investigators will focus on the perceptions of the employer and treatment of the employee to determine whether a violation has occurred. The guidelines also clarify the following definitions:

- *Impairment* means a disorder affecting one or more body systems or a mental disorder, *excluding* environmental, cultural, and economic disadvantages; homosexuality; pregnancy; physical characteristics; common personality traits; and normal deviations in height, weight, or strength. The term also includes medical conditions associated with age (such as hearing loss or arthritis), but not advanced age alone. Post-traumatic stress disorder is considered a covered mental impairment. Obesity is generally not covered, but a body weight of 100 percent over the normal weight is considered an impairment.

- *Substantially limiting* means preventing or significantly restricting a person's ability to perform a major life activity as compared with an average person or to do a class of jobs or a broad range of jobs in varying classes. If an impairment prevents a worker from performing only one particular job, or a narrow range of jobs, the worker is not considered substantially limited in the life activity of working. Chronic or episodic disorders that are substantially limiting when active, however, may be considered disabilities.

- *Major life activities* include such mental and emotional processes as thinking, concentrating, and interacting with other people. These activities are in addition to those listed in previous EEOC regulations: caring for oneself, performing manual tasks, walking, seeing, hearing, speaking, breathing, learning, working, sitting, standing, and lifting.

- *Being regarded as having an impairment* means a person who has an impairment that does not substantially limit a major life activity, but who is treated by an employer as having such a limitation; the impairment substantially limits a major life activity only because of the attitudes of others; or no impairment at all, but is treated by an employer as having a substantially limiting impairment.

Recent Developments in Defining Disability

A nurse who requested two months of unpaid leave to recuperate following abdominal surgery was not disabled under either the ADA or the Rehabilitation Act, the Third Circuit has ruled.[326] The Eighth Circuit has ruled that infertility is not a protected disability under the ADA.[327] A woman who was denied insurance coverage for infertility treatments sued, arguing that the denial constituted discrimination on the basis of disability. The federal appeals court ruled in favor of the employer. Infertility is not a disability under the ADA because procreation is not a major life activity, the court reasoned. Procreation is not listed among the examples of major life activities described in EEOC regulations, and infertility does not interfere with the ability to perform any listed activity, including working, the court explained.[328]

A hospital that fired a nurse after she completed a drug rehabilitation program did not violate the ADA because the nurse was a current drug user, the Fourth Circuit has ruled.[329] After a nurse admitted her addiction to a narcotic, a hospital placed her on a medical leave of absence and helped her report to a drug rehabilitation facility while it continued to investigate her conduct. The day after the nurse completed the inpatient portion of her drug rehabilitation program, the hospital terminated her employment for gross misconduct involving the diversion of controlled substances. The nurse sued the hospital, claiming that she was unlawfully discriminated against on the basis of a disability—her former drug addiction. She contended that she was protected by the ADA because she was not a current drug user. Affirming the trial court, the Fourth Circuit ruled that the nurse was not protected by the ADA because she was currently using illegal drugs when the hospital fired her. The appeals court rejected the nurse's argument that she was not a current drug user when the hospital fired her because she was not using drugs at the precise time of her discharge but was participating in a drug rehabilitation program. The court established that "currently" means a periodic or ongoing activity in which a person engages (even if doing something else at the precise moment) that has not permanently ended. Applying a literal definition of "currently" would produce absurd results, the court noted. For example, an employer could fire a drug using employee only where the employer catches the employee during the act and terminates the employee on the spot. The court further emphasized that the ADA's legislative history and the EEOC's technical assistance manual support a broader meaning of "currently" than advocated by the nurse.

The new EEOC Enforcement Guidance attempts to clarify the status of psychological impairments under the ADA.[330] According to the Enforcement Guidance, traits and behaviors alone are not considered impairments. An EEOC enforcement guidance emphasizes that although traits or behaviors, such as stress, chronic lateness, or poor judgment in themselves are not mental impairments, they may be related to a mental or physical impairment. It is also important to distinguish between temporary conditions and chronic episodic disorders. Temporary conditions that do not have permanent or long-term effects on an individual's major life activities are not substantially limiting. For example, an employee who was distressed for about a month after the end of a romantic relationship but continued his daily routine does not have a disability for the purposes of the ADA. Although the individual had an impairment, the impairment was short-term and did not significantly restrict his major life activities. In contrast, chronic episodic conditions, such as bipolar disorder or major depression, may be substantially limiting impairments if they are substantially limiting when active or have or are likely to recur in substantially limiting forms. Other impairments, such as the ability to interact with others, ability to concentrate, ability to care for himself or herself, and inability to sleep may be substantially limiting if they create a significant restriction compared to the rest of the population.

Courts have split on whether a disability that can be controlled with medications is considered a disability under the ADA, in spite of the EEOC's guidance on the impact of medication on a disability claim. The EEOC's interpretive guidance provides that determining whether an individual is substantially limited in a major life activity must be made without regard to mitigating measures such as medicines or assistive or prosthetic devices. The EEOC cites examples of individuals with impairments such as epilepsy or diabetes that substantially limit life activities. According to the EEOC, these individuals are disabled, even if medication controls the effects of the impairments.[331]

Several courts have followed the EEOC's interpretive guidance. Courts have given deference to the EEOC's regulations in finding that impairments such as Graves' disease and nearsightedness substantially limit a major life activity in spite of the mitigating effects of medication. These courts have also cited the ADA's legislative history, which makes specific reference to the fact that the mitigating effects of medication or prosthetic devices should be ignored when making a disability determination, as further support for their conclusion.[332]

Alternatively, other courts have differed with the EEOC's guidelines, ruling that an impairment that can be controlled with medication is not a disability under the ADA. A federal trial court in Kansas has ruled that an individual whose hypertension was controlled by medication was not disabled under the ADA. Although agency interpretations must be given deference, the court noted, the EEOC's interpretation on whether the mitigating effects of medication should be considered in making a disability determination is in direct conflict with the ADA's statutory requirement to demonstrate that an impairment "substantially limits" their lives. The court reasoned that an insulin-dependant diabetic who can control her condition with insulin or a near-sighted person who can correct her vision with eyeglasses cannot argue that her life is substantially limited by her condition.[333]

Asymptomatic HIV infection is not a disability covered by the ADA. The full membership of the Fourth Circuit found that the plain meaning of the ADA revealed that HIV infection is not an impairment, noting that an infection without any symptoms does not have a diminishing effect on an individual.[334]

Who Is Otherwise Qualified?

A "qualified individual" is defined as "an individual with a disability who satisfies the requisite skill, experience, and educational requirements of the employment position such individual holds or desires, and who, with or without reasonable accommodation, can perform the essential functions of such position."[335] A qualified individual with a disability does not include individuals currently engaging in the use of illegal drugs.[336] However, a qualified individual with a disability does include an individual who has successfully completed a supervised drug rehabilitation program or is otherwise rehabilitated and not using drugs, is participating in a drug rehabilitation program and is not using drugs, or is erroneously regarded as engaging in drug use.[337]

Determining whether an individual is "qualified" for a position is a two-step process, according to the EEOC's interpretive guidance to the ADA.[338] First, the employer should determine whether the individual has the appropriate qualifications for the position. Depending on the position, the job might require an appropriate educational background, employment experience, skills, or licenses. Second, the employer must determine whether the individual can perform the essential functions of the position, with or without reasonable accommodation.

Recent Developments in Identifying Who Is Otherwise Qualified

Employers have avoided liability under the ADA by showing that an employee is not qualified for employment. A radiology aide who missed 82 days of work in a period of about two years could not sue a hospital for discharging him because he was not otherwise qualified for the job, according to a federal trial court decision affirmed by the Third Circuit.[339] In response to the aide's absenteeism and lateness, the hospital took escalating disciplinary measures, finally terminating the employee. The employee sued under the ADA, alleging that the employer discriminated against him by failing to make reasonable accommodations, explaining that his absences were caused by the pain and recurrent pneumonia associated with sickle cell anemia. The hospital defended that the employee was not qualified for the position of radiology aide because he could not regularly attend work, an essential function of the job. The federal trial court agreed with the hospital. Absences caused by a disability do not eliminate the requirement of regular attendance as a job qualification. In this case there are no reasonable accommodations possible, the court noted, because the hospital would have to find other employees to perform the aide's job functions on numerous and unpredictable occasions. Concluding that the aide's frequent absenteeism and lateness precluded ADA protection, the court ruled in favor of the hospital.

An ex-employee at a hospital's chemical dependency center, who suffered a relapse in his drug abuse problems while working at the center, failed to establish that the hospital violated the ADA by discharging him, a federal district court in Mississippi has ruled.[340] As an adolescent marketing representative for the hospital's chemical dependency center, the employee's duties were essentially to solicit patients for the center by calling upon persons who normally refer adolescents for drug abuse treatment, including schools, churches, pastors, and youth court judges. The employee also performed initial interviews and assessments of prospective patients. After working at the center for one year, the employee informed his supervisors that he had suffered a relapse of his drug abuse problems. He subsequently enrolled in a drug treatment program, and upon return to the hospital three weeks later, was terminated from his job. He sued, claiming that he was a "qualified individual with a disability" under the ADA, and that the hospital violated that Act in discharging him on the basis of his chemical dependency problem.

In dismissing the suit, the court found that because the hospital's decision to terminate the employee was made and communicated to the employee before he went into treatment, the employee was not a "qualified individual with a disability" within the meaning of the ADA. Although the ADA excludes from its definition of a disabled individual any employee or applicant who is currently engaging in illegal drug use, it does cover a chemically dependent person who is "participating in a supervised rehabilitation program and is no longer engaging in such use." The court rejected the employee's contention that he was covered under the ADA by reason of this exception. Relying on evidence that the employee was aware of the hospital's decision to discharge him from his position before he entered a drug treatment program, the court reasoned that the employee did not meet the exception criteria of either enrollment in a program or a drug-free lifestyle. The court thus concluded that the employee was a person currently engaging in the illegal use of drugs, and therefore was not protected under the ADA. Noting that the ADA's "safe harbor" for recovering illegal drug users provides coverage only in situations of "long-term abstinence from drug use," the court held that the Act was not intended to protect a relapsed drug user who has not been in recovery long enough to become stable. The court also agreed with the hospital's position that it was essential to the performance of the marketing representative's job not to be a recently relapsed drug abuser, and thus concluded that the employee was not a "qualified individual" because he was unable to perform the essential functions of his job.

Reasonable Accommodations

Generally defined, reasonable accommodation refers to any change in the work environment or in the customary way of doing things that enables an individual with a disability to perform a particular job's functions.[341] Under EEOC regulations, reasonable accommodation can be broken down into the following three categories:

1. measures required to ensure equal opportunity in the application process
2. measures that enable employees to perform the essential functions of a position

3. measures that enable employees with disabilities to enjoy
the same "benefits and privileges" of employment as are
enjoyed by employees without disabilities[342]

Thus, in addition to the requirement that work areas be
accessible, the reasonable accommodation provision requires
employers to make accessible those nonwork areas that are used
for socializing, recreation, and training. Job restructuring may
be mandated as a "reasonable" accommodation; however, such
a requirement will not apply to essential job functions. In addition, in certain situations, employers will be allowed to reassign
a disabled worker to a lower level position, but only "if there are
no accommodations that would enable the employee to remain
in the current position and there are no vacant equivalent positions for which the individual is qualified with or without
accommodation."[343]

The ADA does not require a hospital to transfer a hemodialysis nurse with severely impaired hearing to the orthopaedics
unit, the Seventh Circuit has ruled, because the nurse refused
the hospital's other offers of accommodation.[344] Within six
weeks of being hired to a hospital's hemodialysis unit, a nurse
realized he could not continue, as he could not distinguish
between different types of medical equipment alarms, had difficulty setting up the dialysis machines, and had trouble determining appropriate treatments in certain critical situations. The
nurse requested transfer to the orthopaedics unit where he also
had been offered a position. The hospital refused, instead offering the nurse the choice of additional hemodialysis training,
resigning and reapplying for a different position, or being terminated. The nurse rejected the first two options and was fired.
He sued the hospital under the ADA, arguing that its adherence
to a policy of refusing transfers during the first six months of
employment violated the federal antidiscrimination statute.
The court rejected that argument and ruled in favor of the
hospital. The ADA does not require an employer to provide
everything a disabled employee wants, the court cautioned,
only reasonable accommodations. Reassignment is not required under the ADA but is one of the potential alternatives

that an employer may offer. Here, the hospital offered additional training or the opportunity to reapply for a different position; thus satisfying the employer's duty under the ADA.

A hospital did not discriminate against a maintenance worker on the basis of alcoholism when it demoted him after he was convicted of driving under the influence of alcohol, the Seventh Circuit has ruled.[345]

The ADA does not require employers to make reasonable accommodations for disabled employees if the accommodation violates a bona fide seniority system under a collective bargaining agreement, according to the Seventh Circuit.[346] In this case, a unionized railroad worker with epilepsy could not bump a more senior bargaining unit member from a shift during daytime hours in an office at ground level.

The ADA does not require employers to grant unpaid leave indefinitely, the Tenth Circuit has ruled.[347]

An employee cannot sue for disability discrimination under the ADA unless she shows that she suffered a "materially adverse" employment action, the Sixth Circuit has ruled.[348] A nurse employed by a nursing institution was demoted from supervisor to unit nurse. However, she performed similar job duties, retained the same rate of pay, and later was granted a raise. When the nurse sued, claiming that the job change constituted disability discrimination, the court ruled for the facility because the nurse failed to demonstrate that she suffered any materially adverse job action.

Any conflict between a collective bargaining agreement and an accommodation under the ADA does not prevent an employee from seeking a reasonable accommodation under the ADA, the D.C. Circuit has held. An orderly at a hospital took a medical leave of absence after undergoing heart surgery. When the employee's physician detailed him to light duty work, he started to look for a new job at the hospital that would be consistent with this limitation. The employee applied for several jobs at the hospital but was not selected for any of the jobs. The hospital's collective bargaining agreement contained provisions that required the hospital to post job openings, give preference to employees with greater seniority, and transfer handicapped employees. The orderly sued the hospital, alleging that it failed to reasonable accommodate his disability in violation of the ADA. A federal trial court dismissed the claim, finding that reassigning the orderly to a vacant nonstrenuous position would have violated the seniority provision contained in the collective bargaining agreement. Rejecting this holding, the D.C. Circuit found that the collective bargaining agreement is just one of the factors used to evaluate whether a requested accommodation is reasonable. Examining the orderly's case, the court found that the conflict between the collective bargaining agreement and the duty to make a reasonable accommodation was relatively minor. Accordingly, the D.C. Circuit reinstated the orderly's lawsuit.[349]

An individual who is regarded as disabled but is not actually disabled is not entitled to reasonable accommodation under the ADA. When a nurse who had injured her wrist returned to work after a year's absence due to her injury, she requested a light duty position. The hospital determined that the nurse could not be accommodated in her previous job or any other available job at the hospital and informed her that she could not return to work. The nurse argued on appeal that although she was not disabled, the hospital violated the ADA by firing her because of her perceived disability and by failing to accommodate her lifting restriction. The Third Circuit concluded that Congress did not intend that an individual with only a perceived disability be entitled to accommodation. The court reasoned that providing accommodation to an individual with a perceived disability would give this individual an undeserved windfall because he or she would have a right to accommodation by virtue of the employer's misperception while others with the same impairment would not. In addition, any employee, disabled or not, must be able to perform all functions of a job unless he or she is entitled to accommodation under the ADA. The nurse admitted that the could not perform the job without accommodation. Therefore, the Third Circuit concluded that the nurse was not a qualified individual with a disability and could not maintain her ADA claim.[350]

Application and Interview Questions

The EEOC's Office of Legal Counsel has issued an Enforcement Guidance to EEOC investigators, addressing the legality of preemployment inquiries under the ADA.[351] Although the guidance does not bind employers in the same manner as a law or regulation, employers should note that EEOC investigators will rely on the guidance to determine whether the employer has violated the ADA by improperly questioning a job applicant. The "guiding principle" is that employers may inquire about applicants' ability to perform job functions but may not inquire about disabilities or reasonable accommodations before making a conditional job offer. The guidance addresses the legality of specific questions. For example:

- An employer may not ask, "Do you have a disability that would interfere with your ability to perform the job?" because the question impermissibly seeks information about a disability. An employer may ask, however, "Can you perform the functions of this job with or without reasonable accommodation?" because the question properly focuses on job functions. Employers may ask applicants to describe or demonstrate how they could perform particular job functions under certain circumstances.

- Prior to making a conditional job offer, an employer may not ask, "Would you need reasonable accommodation in this job?" Even if the applicant volunteers a need for reasonable accommodation, the employer may not ask, "What kind of reasonable accommodation would you need for this job?"

- Although employers may not ask, "How many days were you sick last year?" because the question is likely to elicit information regarding a disability, employers may inquire about job applicants' attendance by asking, "Can you meet the attendance requirements of this job?" or "How many days did you take leave last year?"

- An employer may ask, "Are you currently illegally using drugs?" because current illegal drug use is not protected by the ADA. The employer may also ask, "Have you ever illegally used drugs?" but may not inquire into the extent of the prior use, or ask, "Have you ever been treated for drug addiction?" because drug addiction is a protected disability. Further, the employer may not ask, "What medications are you currently taking?" because the question is likely to elicit information about a disability.

- Employers may ask job applicants lifestyle questions such as, "Do you regularly eat three meals per day?" or "How much do you weigh?" or "Do you drink alcohol?" Employers who ask such questions must take care not to ask questions that are likely to elicit information about a disability, such as "How much alcohol do you drink per week?" or "Do you drink alone?"

- Employers may not ask, "Do you have AIDS?" or "Are you an alcoholic?" even if either condition would make the applicant ineligible for the job. Employers are permitted to ask about impairments that are not disabilities, however. For example, an employer may ask a job applicant, "How did you break your leg?" The employer may not go on to ask about the severity and duration of the injury, however, because such questions are likely to disclose whether the applicant has a disability.

Insurance

Health care employers should review employer-provided health insurance plans for possible ADA violations. According to EEOC interim enforcement guidance,[352] a term or a provision of a health plan will violate the ADA if it is a disability-based distinction that is not protected under the ADA. The ADA protects disability-based distinctions contained in a bona fide health insurance plan that are not used as a subterfuge to evade the purposes of the ADA.[353] A term or provision is disability based if it refuses to cover or provides reduced coverage for a particular disability, a discrete group of disabilities, or debility in general (i.e., all conditions that substantially limit a major life activity). Proving that the distinction is not a subterfuge could be difficult for employers, given the EEOC's position that "subterfuge" refers to disability-based disparate treatment not justified by the risks or costs associated with the disability. The guidelines provide some illustrations of potential justifications for such distinctions, including proof that other conditions with comparable actuarial data or experience are treated similarly under the plan. An employer also could justify a disability-based distinction by proving that the provision is necessary to prevent an unacceptable change in the plan's coverage, premiums, copayments, or deductibles. An "unacceptable change" must be either a drastic increase in premiums, copayments, or deductibles, or a drastic modification of the scope of coverage or level of benefits.

Recent Developments in Insurance

Recent cases have not definitively settled how the ADA applies to employer–provider insurance. The ADA does not protect a fired employee after his employer capped his health benefits for AIDS-related treatment, the Eleventh Circuit has ruled.[354] A fired employee elected to continue his health coverage pursuant to the Consolidated Omnibus Budget Reconciliation Act of 1985 (COBRA). Shortly thereafter, his former employer imposed a cap on AIDS-related treatment. The Eleventh Circuit upheld the trial court's dismissal of the lawsuit brought by the former employee, holding that the ADA does not entitle a former employee to protection. Based on the plain language of the ADA, the court concluded that Congress intended to limit the scope of the ADA to only qualified individuals with a disability. The ADA defines qualified individuals with a disability as job applicants and current employees capable of performing essential functions of an available job. The former employee was not a qualified individual with a disability, the court reasoned, because he neither held nor desired to hold a position with his former employer when the former employer capped his health insurance benefits.[355]

Title III of the ADA does not prohibit an employer from providing a disability plan that contains longer benefits for employees disabled because of a physical illness than for those disabled due to a mental illness, the entire membership of the

Sixth Circuit ruled.[356] An employee whose disability benefits ended after 24 months filed suit under the ADA against the insurance company that provided the insurance policy to her employer. A three-judge panel of the Sixth Circuit concluded that Title III prohibits disability discrimination in insurance products because insurance is a good or service provided by a person who owns a public accommodation. The full membership of the court rejected the panel's decision. A benefit plan offered by an employer is not a good offered by a place of public accommodation because a public accommodation is a physical place, the court decided. In addition, the disability policy is not offered by a place of public accommodation, the court reasoned, because the public cannot enter the insurance company's or employer's office and obtain the disability policy that the employee obtained. Because the employee obtained her benefits through her employer and not from the insurer's office, the court found no nexus between the disparity in benefits and the insurance services offered to the public. Therefore, a long-term disability plan offered by an employer is not covered by Title III of the ADA, the full court concluded.

However, an employer that changed group health plans to an insurer that would not cover a disabled group member because of his disability violated the ADA because it did not provide equal access to insurance, a Texas federal trial court has held.[357]

A hospital nurse who was denied family health coverage by the hospital and its benefits administrator may not sue the administrator for discrimination under the ADA, a federal district court in Ohio has ruled.[358] In so holding, the court concluded that any discrimination claim that the nurse has under the ADA must be asserted against the hospital as her employer. The hospital and its benefits administrator denied the nurse's application for family health insurance coverage. The nurse alleged that she was informed that she was eligible for approval for individual coverage, but that family coverage would not be approved because her husband was receiving medication for hypertension and her son was a paraplegic. She sued both the hospital and the administrator, claiming that they engaged in discriminatory behavior in violation of the ADA by denying her family coverage. In dismissing the case, the court rejected the nurse's argument that, by denying her family health insurance benefits, the hospital and the administrator had violated Title III of the ADA. Title III prohibits discrimination on the basis of disability, which prevents the disabled person from equal enjoyment of goods, services, or other accommodations of any place of public accommodation. Although both hospitals and insurance offices can be places of public accommodation subject to Title III, the court nonetheless concluded that these entities do not fall within the meaning of that section in regard to their provision of health insurance benefits and services. The reference throughout that Title makes it clear that its scope is limited to discrimination in the provision of services, facilities, or accommodations based on the disabled person's physical ability to make use of those services, the court explained. Noting that the nurse's claim has nothing to do with an inability to make physical use of the services of a place of public accommodation, the court concluded that there is no nexus between the alleged discrimination and any public accommodation. The court also declined to defer to Justice Department regulations construing Title III as applicable to the sale of insurance contracts. Not only is there no indication in the statutory language that Title III applies to insurance contracts, but Congress has unambiguously expressed its intent that Title III be limited to claims involving the "physical" use of a place of public accommodation, the court reasoned.

Enforcement and Remedies

The EEOC is charged with enforcing the ADA. Because the ADA's prohibitions are substantively similar to those found in the Rehabilitation Act, the EEOC and Department of Justice have issued regulations establishing complaint processing procedures for claims of employment discrimination on the basis of disability.

The EEOC will investigate claims of disability discrimination filed under Title I of the ADA. The remedies and procedures for ADA claims are the same as those under Title VII.[359] If after investigation, the Attorney General has reasonable cause to find a pattern or practice of ADA violation, or a violation of general public importance, the Attorney General may file an action in federal court seeking injunctive relief, compensatory damages, and/or a monetary penalty.[360] Under the Civil Rights Act of 1991, employees with ADA claims have the right to a jury trial, and may recover compensatory damages for pain and suffering, in addition to punitive damages if the employer acted maliciously or recklessly.

Recent Developments in Remedies

The cap on compensatory and punitive damages awarded under the ADA applies to the sum of both types of damages, not to each type independently, the First Circuit has ruled.[361] A railroad employee sued under the ADA, alleging discrimination on the basis of disability, and won a jury verdict for $200,000 in compensatory damages, and $200,000 in punitive damages, as well as back pay. The trial court reduced the award of compensatory and punitive damages to a total of $200,000, reasoning that the ADA itself contains a $200,000 cap on such damages. The employee appealed, interpreting the statute to separately limit each type of damage to $200,000. The First Circuit dismissed the argument as "improbable." The ADA is "clear on its face" that the sum of compensatory and punitive damages cannot exceed $200,000, the court ruled.

Circuit courts of appeal as well as lower district courts are split on the issue of whether personal liability may be imposed on supervisory personnel under antidiscrimination statutes. At least four circuits have held that personal liability may not be imposed against individual management employees under Title VII and the ADEA.[362] At least two other circuits have ruled in favor of individual liability under these statutes.[363] In the first appellate court case to address the issue with respect to the ADA, the U.S. Court of Appeals for the Seventh Circuit has ruled that an employee discharged after informing his employers of his inoperable brain cancer cannot sue the supervisor for discriminatory behavior in violation of the ADA.[364] In so holding, the appeals court resolved a split among the lower courts of the Northern District of Illinois as to whether personal liability may be imposed against supervisors and management personnel under the ADA. A year after the employee was hired to be executive director of a security systems company, he informed his supervisor, the owner of the company, that he had lung cancer. Despite his worsening condition, including a diagnosis of inoperable metastatic brain cancer, the director remained in his full-time position for the next five years. Shortly after the company owner died, his wife took over ownership responsibilities and discharged the director, who subsequently filed a complaint with the EEOC. The EEOC sued both the company and the company's new owner for discriminatory conduct in violation of the ADA.

In reversing the district court's finding of individual liability under the ADA, the Seventh Circuit held that individuals, such as the director's supervisor, who do not independently meet the ADA's definition of "employer" cannot be held liable for ADA violations. The ADA provides that a "covered entity" is prohibited from discriminating on the basis of disability; "entity" is defined as "a person engaged in an industry affecting commerce who has 15 or more employees . . . and any agent of such person." The appeals court rejected the lower court's conclusion that the incorporation of the term "agent" within the ADA's definition of employers indicates that individuals are subject to liability for engaging in unlawful employment discrimination. To the contrary, the "agent" language was included in the statute to ensure that courts would hold corporate and institutional employers responsible for their employees' actions taken on their behalf, or, in other words, would impose *respondeat superior* liability on employers whose agents violated the ADA, the court reasoned. Finding this interpretation to be in accordance with the rest of the ADA's structure, the court observed that Congress intended to limit employer liability under the ADA so as to protect small entities from the hardship of litigating discrimination claims, and thus could not have meant for the statute to allow civil liability to run against individual employees. The court also rejected the argument that imposition of individual liability is essential to achieving the full deterrent effect of the ADA. Declining to disturb Congress's attempt to structure the statute to achieve a balance between deterrence and societal costs, the court concluded that liability imposed on the employing entity is a sufficient incentive to adequately discipline employees for unlawful discrimination. The court thus held the employer, and not the supervisor, responsible for payment of compensatory and punitive damages to the discharged employee.[365]

CIVIL RIGHTS ACT OF 1991

On November 21, 1991, President Bush signed the Civil Rights Act of 1991,[366] ending nearly two years of debate over this controversial piece of legislation. The Act implements significant changes to Title VII of the Civil Rights Act of 1964 and to Section 1981 of the Civil Rights Act of 1866 by reversing several recent Supreme Court rulings that narrowed their scope. In particular, the Act reverses the Court's ruling in *Wards Cove Packing Co. v. Atonio*[367] that requires an employee to prove lack of business justification for an employer's facially neutral practice that causes an unlawful disparate impact. The Act stipulates that once an employee has proven the existence of such a business practice, the employer must prove that the practice is job-related for the position in question and consistent with business necessity. In addition, the practice may be unlawful even if the employer succeeds in demonstrating business necessity, if the employee is able to establish that an alternative employment practice with less disparate impact exists but that the employer has refused to adopt it.[368] The Act also overrules *Price Waterhouse v. Hopkins*,[369] by providing that an employer commits an unlawful employment practice if an employee demonstrates that race, color, sex, religion, or national origin was a motivating factor in an adverse employment decision, even though other factors also motivated the decision.[370] In addition, the Act reverses *Lorance v. AT& T*,[371] stating that the filing period for challenging an allegedly discriminatory seniority system under Title VII begins to run when the system is adopted, when the employee falls within the scope of the system, or when the employee is injured by application of the system, whichever date is the most beneficial to the employee.[372] Finally, the Act also sweeps aside the Supreme Court's ruling in *Patterson v. McLean Credit Union*[373] by prohibiting under Section

1981 of the 1866 Civil Rights Act discrimination in all phases of employment, not only discrimination in hiring.[374]

Another significant feature of the Act is the extension of damages to victims of intentional gender, religious, and disability discrimination under Title VII, the ADA, and Section 501 of the Rehabilitation Act.[375] Previously, only victims of intentional racial or ethnic discrimination were entitled to compensatory and punitive damages. Under the Act, compensatory damages may be recovered in suits against private employers, state and local governments, or the federal government in cases of intentional discrimination. Nonpublic employers may also be liable for punitive damages but only if the employer acted with malice or reckless indifference to a victim's rights. Most compensatory and all punitive damage awards are capped at $50,000 for employers of 100 or fewer employees, $100,000 for employers with more than 100 and fewer than 201 employees, $200,000 for employers with more than 200 and fewer than 501 employees, and $300,000 for employers of more than 500 workers. The Act also allows any party to demand a jury trial in cases in which compensatory or punitive damages are sought.[376] In cases where the charge of discrimination involves a failure to reasonably accommodate a disabled individual pursuant to the ADA or the Rehabilitation Act, an employer may avoid liability for compensatory or punitive damages by demonstrating that it made good-faith efforts to accommodate the disability. Good-faith efforts must include consultation with the disabled individual.[377]

The Act provides that it and its amendments shall take effect upon enactment.[378] The Act also includes another provision, however, that specifically exempts from the terms of the law a well-known then-pending case involving the Wards Packing Company.[379] In accordance with President Bush's signing statement that the new Civil Rights Act was not retroactive, the EEOC has issued a policy guide declaring that the compensatory and punitive damages provisions of the law apply only to cases of intentionally discriminatory conduct that occurred after the Act's effective date.[380]

The Supreme Court has resolved a split among the circuit courts regarding the retroactive application of the Act, declaring that the statute applies only prospectively.[381] The case involved a claim for discriminatory discharge under Section 1981. A circuit court dismissed suit because of the previous Supreme Court ruling in *Patterson v. McClean Credit Union*,[382] which declared that Section 1981's prohibition on racial discrimination applies only to conduct that occurs before an employment contract is established. Although the Civil Rights Act of 1991 specifically overrules the *Patterson* decision, applying the prohibition on discrimination to all phases of the contractual relationship between employer and employee, the provision did not apply to this case, the Court held, because it arose before the statute was enacted. Unlike earlier versions of the law, the Civil Rights Act of 1991 as enacted does not declare that its purpose is to restore protections that the *Patterson* decision had eliminated. The fact that the law was enacted in response to *Patterson* does not supply sufficient evidence that Congress intended to override the presumption against statutory retroactivity, the Court concluded.

FAMILY AND MEDICAL LEAVE ACT

On February 5, 1993, President Clinton signed the Family and Medical Leave Act (FMLA) into law.[383] The Act preempts state and local laws, unless they provide greater leave rights. It applies to all private employers with 50 or more employees within a 75-mile radius of the work site, as well as to federal civil service and state and local government employees.[384] For nonunionized employers, the Act became effective on August 6, 1993. For employers with collective bargaining agreements, however, the Act begins to apply either on the date the contract expires or one year after the date of enactment, whichever is earlier.[385]

Under the Act, employers must provide up to 12 weeks of leave per year for an employee's serious illness, the birth or adoption of a child, or caring for a sick spouse, child, or parent.[386] In addition, employers are required to grant the same amount of leave to employees who suffer a serious health condition and are unable to perform their duties.[387] To be eligible for leave under the Act, an employee must have been employed for at least 12 months at the time the leave is requested, and have completed at least 1,250 hours of service with such employer during the previous 12-month period.[388] Employers must guarantee that employees on leave will return to the same or comparable position if they return to work within the maximum allowable leave period.[389] An employer may refuse to restore an employee to a former position if the employee is salaried and among the highest paid 10 percent of the employer's work force, and the refusal is necessary to prevent substantial economic injury to the employer. Significantly, the Act also requires employers to maintain health care coverage during the leave on the same basis and under the same condition as if the employee was not on leave status.[390]

The Department of Labor has issued interim final rules implementing the FMLA.[391] Significant provisions in the rules include:

- A definition of "serious health condition." This includes any period of inpatient care in a hospital or residential facility; any period of incapacity requiring absence from work for three or more calendar days and involving continuing treatment by a health care provider, any chronic long-term health condition that is incurable or serious and that requires continuing treatment by a health care provider, or continuing prenatal care by a health care provider. Treatment for allergies, stress, or substance abuse could also be a "serious health condition," but most elective or cosmetic treatments would not be.[392]

- Entitlement rules. An employer can choose among several ways to calculate which 12-month period will be used to determine entitlement to the 12 workweeks of leave allowed under the FMLA. These include the calendar year, an employer-designated 12-month leave year, a 12-month period measured from the day any employee's FMLA leave begins, or a rolling 12-month period calculated backward from the date an employee uses any FMLA leave.[393]

- Provisions governing intermittent and reduced leave. Although there is no limit on the size of a leave increment, an employer may limit leave increments to the shortest time period used by its payroll system to monitor absences. Intermittent or reduced leave must be medically necessary, and not simply based on child care concerns. [394]

Recent Developments under the Family and Medical Leave Act

The Department of Labor's final regulations implementing the FMLA are now effective.[395] The final regulations clarify the following issues:

- Covered employers. Employers that employ 50 or more employees for 20 or more workweeks per year are covered by FMLA. Employees at separate work sites are counted if the sites are within 75 miles, measured by the shortest route in surface miles. Employers should count jointly employed workers, such as workers placed with the employer (the secondary employer) by a temporary agency (the primary employer).

- Definition of "serious health condition." A serious health condition for which FMLA leave must be granted includes conditions that require inpatient care or continuing treatment by a health care provider. To qualify for FMLA leave under the "continuing treatment" provision, an employee must show a period of incapacity of more than three consecutive days, as well as two or more treatments by a health care provider, or one treatment as part of a continuing treatment regimen, such as for pregnancy, asthma, and Alzheimer's disease. Employees also are eligible for FMLA leave for any period of absence to receive treatments for conditions that would result in more than three days incapacity in the absence of treatment, such as chemotherapy for cancer.

- Illegal drug use. Substance abuse may qualify as a serious health condition. FMLA leave may be taken only for treatment, however, if the treatment is administered by a health care provider, or by a provider of health services on referral by a health care provider. Absence because of substance use, rather than treatment, does not qualify for FMLA leave.

- Definition of health care provider. This term includes not only physicians, but all providers "capable of providing health care services," including nurse practitioners, clinical social workers, and any provider from whom the employer's health insurance plan will accept certification of a serious health condition.

Current case law provides guidance about what constitutes a serious health condition under the FMLA. Courts have ruled that the following illnesses do not meet the FMLA's definition of a serious health condition

- sinobronchitis[396]
- rectal bleeding[397]
- food poisoning that required one visit to the doctor[398]
- gastroenteritis and upper respiratory infection where there was no proof that the patient was incapacitated for more than three calendar days[399]
- asthma[400]
- ear infection[401]

CONFLICT OF LAWS

The interaction of the ADA, FMLA, and workers' compensation raises several leave issues. The ADA, FMLA, state workers' compensation laws, and disability laws such as Social Security may apply when an employee is sick or injured. In particular, these laws raise complicated questions concerning leave and the definition of disability. The convergence of these laws raise complicated issues for employers when they attempt to comply with these laws.

The ADA, FMLA, and state workers' compensation laws may apply when an employee requires time off from work because of a medical condition. Not all employers will be required to comply with all three laws when an employee requires time off because of a medical condition. Although an employer with one employee is a "covered employee" for workers' compensation purposes, the ADA and FMLA have different coverage requirements. Generally, the FMLA applies to employers with 50 or more employees and the ADA applies to an employer with 15 or more employees.

Additionally, not all medical conditions are protected by all three statutes. Workers' compensation applies to an employee's injury or illness that occurs in the course of the job. The FMLA's definition of a serious health condition is broad and covers conditions, such as an overnight hospital stay, that are not covered by the ADA. The ADA provides protection for individuals who suffer from an impairment that affects a major life activity. Additionally, the ADA requires that the employee be able to perform the essential functions of his or her job.

Leave

The interaction of the ADA, FMLA, and workers' compensation raises several leave issues. The FMLA regulations provide that an employee who is receiving workers' compensation because of an on-the-job injury can concurrently take FMLA leave.[402] This option is often attractive to employees because the employee is receiving money as the FMLA only provides for unpaid leave (although employers have the option of allowing employees to take sick or vacation time), the employee is guaranteed to have group coverage continuation under the FMLA, and the FMLA guarantees reinstatement for up to 12 weeks of leave. If an employee refuses light duty during this period, an employer may be able to terminate workers' compensation benefits but the FMLA leave period continues.

It is not clear to what extent time on light duty counts toward the 12-week right to reinstatement or toward the 12 weeks of unpaid leave under the FMLA. The regulations provide that time spent on light duty counts toward the right to reinstatement.[403] However, the regulations are silent on whether time spent on light duty counts toward the 12 weeks of leave, because the employee is working during this time.

Under the ADA, an employer cannot require an employee with an occupational-related injury to be able to return to full duty before allowing him or her to return to work. If an employee on "light duty" can still perform the essential functions of the job with or without a reasonable accommodation that does not pose an undue hardship on the employer, the employee can return to work.[404]

Even after an employee exhausts the 12-week leave period under the FMLA, he or she might be entitled to additional leave under the ADA. A medical leave of absence is one form of reasonable accommodation under the ADA. An otherwise qualified employee with a disability is entitled to additional leave as long as the leave does not pose an undue hardship on the employer.[405] Thus, if the employer determines that it would cause an undue hardship if an employee is out for more than 12 weeks, it can terminate an employee who does not return to work after the 12 weeks of FMLA leave expire. However, the ADA does not require employers to grant unpaid leave indefinitely.[406]

Conflicting Disability Definitions

The interaction of fair employment laws and various disability benefits laws can create confusion in defining disability. The purpose of the ADA, ADEA, and other fair employment laws is to prohibit employers from discriminating against qualified individuals. The purpose of disability benefits and workers' compensation is to provide money to individuals who are disabled as defined by various state and federal laws. The difficulty occurs because employees are claiming that they are disabled and unable to work under the various disability and workers' compensation statutes yet simultaneously claim that they are able to work and are requesting reasonable accommodation under the ADA. Courts and employers are struggling with reconciling the ADA with the various disability benefit laws.

The EEOC recently issued enforcement guidelines about the effect of representations made in applications for disability benefits on an ADA claim. Representations made in an application for disability benefits do not bar an individual from bringing a claim under the ADA, according to the EEOC. Because the definition of disability used in the ADA differs from the way disability benefits programs use the term, an individual can beat the eligibility requirements for disability benefits and still qualify for coverage under the ADA. Unlike other disability determinations, the ADA focuses on what an individual with a disability can do and never presumes that some impairments are so severe that an individual is unable to work. The ADA also requires an individualized assessment about whether a disabled individual is qualified for a specific job as opposed to work in general. In contrast to Social Security and other disability benefits, the ADA requires employers to consider whether an individual with a disability can perform the job at issue with reasonable accommodation. Representations made in disability applications, however, may be relevant to whether the individual is a "qualified individual with a disability" under the ADA. In assigning what weight to give representations made in support of applications for disability benefits, the EEOC has instructed its investigators to examine the context and timing of the representations.[407]

Prior to the EEOC's guidance, however, the majority of courts found that individuals who claim total disability in their applications for disability benefits cannot pursue claims under the ADA as well. For example, the Third Circuit precluded an individual receiving disability benefits from pursuing an ADA claim against his former employer.[408] After the company fired the employee, he applied for state disability benefits, Social Security disability benefits, and an exemption from repayment of a student loan by making sworn statements that he was totally and permanently disabled and unable to work. The employee also sued the company, alleging that it violated the ADA by firing him because he was HIV positive.

The Third Circuit ruled that the employee was precluded from pursuing his ADA claim because he had made sworn statements in his disability benefits applications that he was unable to work due to a total and permanent disability. The court reasoned that the employee was prevented from also arguing that he is a qualified individual who can perform the essential function of his former job. Although the Social Security Administration may have different criteria for disability than the ADA, the court concluded, this does not permit an individual from undermining the judicial system by taking inconsistent positions about his ability to work.[409]

A number of courts, however, have held that the receipt of disability benefits does not prevent an individual from proving that he or she can perform the essential functions of his or her job. An Illinois federal trial court reasoned that Social Security's decision to award benefits does not mean that an employee is not a "qualified individual" with a disability. Similarly, a New York federal trial court noted that an individual may be disabled for purposes of receiving Social Security because of a lack of jobs structured to accommodate his or her disability and may still be protected by the ADA because a particular job could be modified to accommodate the disability.[410]

Using reasoning similar to cases decided under the ADA, several courts have prevented individuals who claimed in applications for disability benefits that they were disabled from proceeding against their former employers on age discrimination claims. A federal trial court in New York ruled that an employee who claimed on his application for Social Security disability benefits that he was totally disabled was prevented from proceeding in a lawsuit against his employer under the ADA.[411] Similarly, the Ninth Circuit ruled that an employee who received a favorable workers' compensation settlement based on her claim that she was unable to work cannot sue her employer under California's age discrimination statute.[412]

EMPLOYEE WAIVERS OF DISCRIMINATION CLAIMS

Recent policy guidance from the EEOC and several federal appeals court decisions address the validity of agreements that waive employees' rights under antidiscrimination statutes. The EEOC has issued a policy guidance stating that an employer may not interfere with the rights of an employee to file a charge, testify, assist, or participate in any EEOC investigation, hearing, or proceeding under Title VII, the ADA, the ADEA, and the EPA. Although a waiver agreement can eliminate an individual's right to personal recovery, it cannot interfere with the EEOC's right to enforce Title VII, the EPA, the ADA, or the ADEA by seeking relief that will benefit the public and any victims who have not validly waived their claims. The EEOC has instructed its investigators to issue a cause determination if a charging party has been required to give up his or her right to file a charge or participate in an investigation by the EEOC.

Several recent decisions by federal circuit courts of appeal discuss the validity of waivers of statutory rights under federal antidiscrimination statutes:

- A union cannot waive employees' rights to litigate federal employment discrimination statutes by signing a collective bargaining agreement that agrees to arbitrate employment-related disputes, the Seventh Circuit has ruled.[413]

- An employee's waiver of his ADA claim in return for certain benefits was valid because it was "knowing and voluntary," the First Circuit has ruled. The court noted that nothing in the ADA prohibits such releases and the ADA's legislative history shows an intent to permit individuals to settle or waive claims under the ADA by express, voluntary agreement.[414]

- An employee's signing of an arbitration clause contained in an employee handbook constitutes a valid agreement to arbitrate her Title VII claims, the Eight Circuit has decided.[415]

- An employee who signed a form agreeing to submit all employment disputes to arbitration must submit her FLMA claim to arbitration, the Fourth Circuit has ruled.[416]

- An employee who agreed to arbitrate his employment-related claims as a condition of his employment must submit his Title VII claim to arbitration, the D.C. Court of Appeals has ruled. The court emphasized that it would only enforce an arbitration agreement if it met minimal standards of procedural fairness, noting that this arbitration arrangement did so because it provided for neutral arbitrators; provided for more than minimal discovery; required a written award; provided for all of the relief that would otherwise be available in court; and did not require employees to pay unreasonable costs or fees or expenses as a condition of access to arbitration.[417]

NOTES

1. 42 U.S.C. §§ 2000e through 2000e-17.
2. 42 U.S.C. §§ 2000e through 2000e-17.
3. 42 U.S.C. § 2000e(b).
4. There is also a limited exemption from the Act for a "bona fide private membership club which is exempt from taxation under Section 501(c)" of Title 26. 42 *U.S.C.* § 2000e(b). A federal district court has ruled that a private nonprofit hospital does not come within the "private club" exemptions of Title VII. *EEOC v. St. Joseph's Hosp. E., Inc.*, No. 79-2033-W (W.D. Tenn. 1979) (unpublished). In addition, a federal trial court has ruled that unpaid volunteers are not protected by Title VII. *Smith v. Berks Community Television*, 657 F. Supp. 794 (E.D. Pa. 1987).
5. 42 U.S.C. § 2000e-2(a).
6. 42 U.S.C. § 2000e-2(d).
7. 42 U.S.C. § 2000e-3(a).
8. 42 U.S.C. § 2000e-3(b).
9. 42 U.S.C. § 2000e(k).
10. *McDonnell Douglas Corp. v. Green*, 411 U.S. 792 (1973).
11. *Robinson v. Shell Oil Co.*, 117 S. Ct. 843 (1997).
12. 42 U.S.C. §§ 2000e-2 & 2000e-3. See, e.g., *DeLesstine v. Fort Wayne State Hosp. & Training Ctr.*, 682 F.2d 130 (7th Cir. cert. denied sub nom. *Ackerman v. DeLesstine*, 459 U.S. 1017 (1982)); *Wrighten v. Metropolitan Hosps., Inc.*, 726 F.2d 1346 (9th Cir. 1984). But see *Beverley v. Douglas*, 591 F. Supp. 1321 (S.D.N.Y. 1984) (appointment to the voluntary attending staff of a hospital not an employment opportunity under Title VII).
13. *Judie v. Hamilton*, 872 F.2d 919 (9th Cir. 1989), cert denied, 515 U.S. 1173 (1995).
14. *Walker v. IRS*, 713 F. Supp. 403 (N.D. Ga. 1989).
15. See, e.g., *Alexander v. Rush N. Shore Medical Ctr.*, 851 F. Supp. 330 (N.D. Ill. 1994), aff'd, 101 F. 3d 487 (7th Cir. 1996).
16. *Griggs v. Duke Power Co.*, 401 U.S. 424 (1971).
17. 42 U.S.C. § 2000e-2(k).
18. 42 U.S.C. § 2000e-2(k).
19. *Kennedy v. Crittenden*, No. 77-200-MAC (D. Ga. Nov. 24, 1982) (unpublished).
20. *United States v. Medical Soc'y of S.C.*, 298 F. Supp. 145 (D.S.C. 1969).
21. *Connecticut v. Teal*, 457 U.S. 440 (1982).
22. *Gregory v. Litton Sys.*, 472 F. 2d 631 (9th Cir. 1972).
23. *Anderson v. HCA Deer Park Hosp.*, 834 F. Supp. 183 (S.D.Tex. 1993).

24. *EEOC v. North Hills Passavant Hosp.*, 466 F. Supp. 783 (W.D. Pa. 1979).

25. 42 U.S.C. § 1981. Section 1982 applies to the sale or rental of property and is not discussed in this manual.

26. *Johnson v. Railway Express Agency, Inc.*, 421 U.S. 454 (1975).

27. *Johnson v. Railway Express Agency, Inc.*, 421 U.S. 454 (1975).

28. *Guerra v. Manchester Terminal Corp.*, 498 F.2d 641 (5th Cir. 1974); but see *De Malherbe v. Int'l Union of Elevator Contractors*, 438 F. Supp. 1121 (N.D.Cal. 1977).

29. *Espinoza v. Farah Mfg. Co.*, 414 U.S. 86 (1973).

30. *St. Francis College v. Al-Khazraji*, 481 U.S. 604 (1987); *Shaare Tefila Congregation v. Cobb*, 481 U.S. 615 (1987).

31. But see *Patee v. Pacific Northwest Bell Tel. Co.*, 803 F.2d 476 (9th Cir. 1986) (male employees cannot sue under Title VII as persons injured because of sex-based wage discrimination against women).

32. 29 C.F.R. §§ 1604.1 through 1604.11.

33. 42 U.S.C. § 2000e-2(e). See *EEOC v. Mercy Hosp. Ctr.*, No. Civ-80-1374-W (W.D. Okla. 1982) (unpublished) (male nurses lawfully barred from assignment in labor and delivery areas because sex-based job qualification justified by nondiscriminatory business reasons or patients' privacy rights); *Jones v. Hinds Gen. Hosp.*, 666 F. Supp. 933 (S.D. Miss. 1987).

34. *AFSCME Local 567 v. Michigan Council 25*, 635 F. Supp. 1010 (E.D. Mich. 1986).

35. 29 C.F.R. § 1604.2(a)(1).

36. See, e.g., *Little Forest Medical Ctr. v. Ohio Civil Rights Comm'n*, 575 N.E.2d 1164 (Ohio 1991), cert. denied, 503 U.S. 906 (1992).

37. *EEOC v. Mercy Health Ctr.*, No. CIV-80-1374-W (W.D. Okla. 1982) (unpublished).

38. *Walker v. St. Anthony's Medical Ctr.*, 881 F.2d 554 (8th Cir. 1989).

39. *Veatch v. Northwestern Memorial Hosp.*, 730 F. Supp. 809 (N.D. Ill. 1990).

40. 42 U.S.C. § 2000e-7.

41. 29 C.F.R. § 1604.2(b)(1); *Weeks v. Southern Bell Tel.*, 408 F.2d 228 (5th Cir. 1969).

42. *Yuhas v. Libbey-Owens-Ford Co.*, 562 F.2d 496 (7th Cir. 1977), cert. denied, 435 U.S. 934 (1978).

43. 29 C.F.R. § 1604.5.

44. 29 C.F.R. § 1604.7.

45. *Bruno v. Crown Point, Ind.*, 950 F.2d 355 (7th Cir. 1991), cert. denied, 505 U.S. 1207 (1992).

46. *County of Wash. v. Gunther*, 452 U.S. 161 (1981).

47. 29 C.F.R. § 1604.9.

48. 29 C.F.R. § 1604.9.

49. *Wambheim v. J.C. Penney Co.*, 705 F.2d 1492 (9th Cir. 1983), cert. denied, 467 U.S. 1255 (1984).

50. *Newport News Shipbuilding & Dry Dock Co. v. EEOC*, 462 U.S. 669 (1983).

51. 29 C.F.R. § 1604.9(f).

52. *Arizona Governing Comm. v. Norris*, 463 U.S. 1073 (1983).

53. *Fleming v. Ayers & Assocs.*, 948 F.2d 993 (6th Cir. 1991).

54. 42 U.S.C. § 2000e(k).

55. *International Union v. Johnson Controls, Inc.*, 499 U.S. 187 (1991). For other rulings on the issue of fetal protection policies, see *Wright v. Olin Corp.*, 697 F.2d 1172 (4th Cir. 1982), on remand 585 F. Supp. 1447 (W.D.N.C. 1984); *Zuniga v. Kleberg County Hosp.*, 692 F.2d 986 (5th Cir. 1982); *Hays v. Shelby Memorial Hosp.*, 726 F.2d 1543 (11th Cir. 1984).

56. *Policy Guidance on the Supreme Court Decision in International Union, United Automobile, Aerospace & Agriculture Implement Workers of America v. Johnson Controls*, EEOC (June 28, 1991).

57. *Doe v. Osteopathic Hosp.*, 333 F. Supp. 1357 (D. Kan. 1971).

58. EEOC Dec. No. 71-332 (Sept. 8, 1970).

59. *Maddox v. Grandview Care Ctr., Inc.*, 607 F. Supp. 1404 (M.D. Ga. 1985), aff'd, 780 F.2d 987 (11th Cir. 1986).

60. *Fields v. Bolger*, 723 F.2d 1216 (6th Cir. 1984).

61. 29 C.F.R. § 1604.10(c).

62. *Scher v. Woodland Sch. Community Consol. Dist. No. 50*, 867 F.2d 974 (7th Cir. 1988).

63. *EEOC v. Warshawski & Co.*, 768 F. Supp. 647 (N.D. Ill. 1991); 29 C.F.R. § 1604.10(c).

64. 29 U.S.C. §§ 2601 through 2654.

65. *California Fed. Sav. & Loan Ass'n v. Guerra*, 479 U.S. 272 (1987).

66. *Newport News Shipbuilding & Dry Dock Co. v. EEOC*, 667 F.2d 448 (4th Cir. 1982).

67. *Newport News Shipbuilding & Dry Dock Co. v. EEOC*, 462 U.S. 669 (1983).

68. *Aubrey v. Aetna Life Ins. Co.*, 886 F.2d 119 (6th Cir. 1989).

69. *EEOC v. Puget Sound Log Scaling & Grading Bureau*, 752 F.2d 1389 (9th Cir. 1985).

70. See, e.g., *Knott v. Missouri Pac. R.R.*, 527 F.2d 1249 (8th Cir. 1975).

71. See, e.g., *Fountain v. Safeway Stores, Inc.*, 555 F.2d 753 (9th Cir. 1977).

72. See, e.g., *Lanigan v. Barlett & Co. Grain*, 466 F. Supp. 1388 (W.D. Mo. 1979).

73. See, e.g., *Carswell v. Peachford Hosp.*, No. C80-222A (N.D. Ga. May 26, 1981) (unpublished).

74. *Carroll v. Tallman Fed. Sav. & Loan Ass'n*, 604 F.2d 1028 (7th Cir. 1979), cert. denied, 445 U.S. 929 (1980).

75. *Lanigan v. Barlett & Co. Grain*, 466 F. Supp. 1388 (W.D. Mo. 1979).

76. See, e.g., *Smith v. Liberty Mut. Life Ins. Co.*, 395 F. Supp. 1098 (N.D. Ga. 1975), aff'd, 569 F.2d 325 (5th Cir. 1978).

77. *Voyles v. Ralph K. Davis Medical Ctr.*, 403 F. Supp. 456 (N.D. Cal. 1975); see also *Willingham v. Macon Tel. Publishing Co.*, 507 F.2d 1084 (5th Cir. 1975).

78. 29 C.F.R. § 1604.11(a).

79. 29 C.F.R. § 1604.11(a).

80. *Karibian v. Columbia Univ.*, 14 F.3d 773 (2d Cir. 1994), cert. denied, 512 U.S. 1213 (1994).

81. *Meritor Sav. Bank v. Vinson*, 477 U.S. 57 (1986).

82. *Harris v. Forklift Sys., Inc.*, 510 U.S. 17 (1993).

83. *Kopp v. Samaritan Health Sys. Inc.*, 13 F.3d 264 (8th Cir. 1993).

84. 29 C.F.R. § 1604.11(c). See also *Toscano v. Nimmo*, 570 F. Supp. 1197 (D. Del. 1983); *Ford v. Revlon, Inc.*, 734 P.2d 580 (Ariz. 1987) (company's failure to take appropriate action after employee lodged sexual harassment charges against supervisor constituted intentional infliction of emotional distress).

85. *Sparks v. Regional Medical Ctr. Bd.*, 792 F. Supp. 735 (N.D. Ala. 1992).

86. See also *Kopp v. Samaritan Health Sys. Inc.*, 13 F.3d 264 (8th Cir. 1993) (trial appropriate where hospital was aware of cardiologist's abusive conduct for years).

87. *Smith v. St. Louis Univ.*, 109 F.3d 1261 (8th Cir. 1997).

88. *Blankenship v. Parke Care Ctrs.*, 123 F.3d 868 (6th Cir. 1997).

89. *Farpella-Crosby v. Horizon Health Care*, 97 F.3d 803 (5th Cir. 1996).

90. *Faragher v. Boca Raton, Fla.*, 111 F.3d 1530 (11th Cir. 1997).

91. *Harrison v. Eddy Potash Inc.*, 112 F.3d 1437 (10th Cir. 1997).

92. *Kolstad v. American Dental Ass'n.*, 108 F.3d 1431 (D.C. Cir. 1997); *Luciano v. Olsten Corp.*, 109 F.3d 111 (2d Cir. 1997).

93. *Healey v. Southwood Psychiatric Hosp.*, 78 F.3d 128 (3d Cir. 1996).

94. *Garcia v. Woman's Hosp.*, 97 F.3d 810 (5th Cir. 1996).

95. *Turic v. Holland Hospitality, Inc.*, 85 F.3d 1211 (6th Cir. 1996).

96. *Armstrong v. Flowers Hosp.*, 33 F.3d 1308 (11th Cir. 1994).

97. *McWilliams v. Fairfax County Bd. of Supervisors*, 72 F.3d 1191 (4th Cir.), cert. denied 117 S. Ct. 72 (1996).

98. *Wrightson v. Pizza Hut*, No. 96-1127 (4th Cir. Oct. 31, 1996).

99. *Quick v. Donaldson Co.*, 90 F.3d 1372 (8th Cir. 1996).

100. *Giddens v. Shell Oil Co.*, 12 F.3d 208 (5th Cir. 1993) (table format), cert. denied, 513 U.S. 925 (1994).

101. *Oncale v. Sundower Offshore Servs.*, 83 F.3d 118 (5th Cir. 1996) cert granted, 1997 U.S. Lexis 3681 (June 9, 1997).

102. *Fredette v. BVP Management Assocs.*, 112 F.3d 1503 (11th Cir. 1997).

103. *Melnychenko v. 84 Lumber Co.*, 676 N.E.2d 45 (Mass. 1997).

104. *Yeary v. Goodwill Indust.*, 107 F.3d 443 (6th Cir. 1997).

105. 29 C.F.R. § 1605.1.

106. *EEOC v. Ithaca Indus., Inc.*, 849 F.2d 116 (4th Cir. 1988), cert. denied, 488 U.S. 924 (1988).

107. *Ansonia Bd. of Educ. v. Philbrook*, 479 U.S. 60 (1986).

108. *Kenny v. Ambulatory Centre of Miami, Inc.*, 400 So. 2d 1262 (Fla. Dist. Ct. App. 1981).

109. *Murphy v. Edge Memorial Hosp.*, 550 F. Supp. 1185 (M.D. Ala. 1982). See also *Pennsylvania State Univ. v. Pennsylvania*, 505 A.2d 1053 (Pa. Commw. Ct. 1986); *Baz v. Walters*, 782 F.2d 701 (7th Cir. 1986).

110. *Smith v. Pyro Mining Co.*, 827 F.2d 1081 (6th Cir. 1987), cert. denied, 485 U.S. 989 (1988).

111. *Hobbie v. Unemployment Appeals Comm'n of Fla.*, 480 U.S. 136 (1987).

112. 42 U.S.C. § 2000e-1(a). See also *Church of Jesus Christ of Latter-Day Saints v. Amos*, 483 U.S. 327 (1987) (religious-owned businesses free to hire only members of their own faith).

113. *Young v. Shawnee Mission Medical Ctr.*, No. 88-2321-S (D. Kan. Oct. 21, 1988) (unpublished).

114. *King's Garden, Inc. v. FCC*, 498 F.2d 51 (D.C. Cir. 1974), cert. denied, 419 U.S. 996 (1974).

115. *EEOC v. Pacific Press Publishing Ass'n.*, 676 F.2d 1272 (9th Cir. 1982).

116. *Trans World Airlines, Inc. v. Hardison*, 432 U.S. 63 (1977).

117. *Guidelines on Religious Expression in the Federal Workplace*, The White House, Aug. 14, 1997.

118. 29 C.F.R. §§ 1606.1 through 1606.8.

119. 29 C.F.R. § 1606.5.

120. *Espinoza v. Farah Mfg. Co., Inc.*, 414 U.S. 86 (1973).

121. See, e.g., *Mass. Ann. Laws*, ch. 149, § 19C.

122. *Garcia v. Rush-Presbyterian-St. Luke's Medical Ctr.*, 660 F.2d 1217 (7th Cir. 1981) (English found to be BFOQ in sophisticated hospital).

123. 29 C.F.R. § 1606.1.

124. 29 C.F.R. § 1606.1.

125. *Dimaranan v. Pomona Valley Hosp. Medical Ctr.*, 775 F. Supp. 338 (C.D. Cal. 1991).

126. *Garcia v. Spun Steak Co.*, 998 F.2d 1480 (9th Cir. 1993), cert. denied, 512 U.S. 1227 (1994).

127. *Hong v. Children's Memorial Hosp.*, 993 F.2d 1257 (7th Cir. 1993), cert. denied, 511 U.S. 1005 (1994).

128. *Amro v. St. Luke's Hosp. of Bethlehem*, Civ. A. No. 84-1355 (E.D. Pa. 1986) (unpublished).

129. *Harmon v. San Diego County*, 477 F. Supp. 1084 (S.D. Cal. 1979).

130. *DeFunis v. Odegaard*, 416 U.S. 312 (1974); *Bakke v. Regents of the Univ. of Calif.*, 553 P.2d 1152 (Cal. 1976), aff'd in part, rev'd in part, 438 U.S. 265 (1978).

131. *Bakke v. Regents of the Univ. of Cal.*, 438 U.S. 265 (1978).

132. *Weber v. Kaiser Aluminum & Chemical Corp.*, 444 U.S. 889 (1979).

133. *Johnson v. Transportation Agency*, 480 U.S. 616 (1987).

134. 29 C.F.R. § 1601.8.

135. 29 C.F.R. § 1601.7.

136. 29 C.F.R. § 1601.13.

137. 29 C.F.R. § 1601.13. For a discussion of the applicability of the 300-day limit when an employee did not file with the state in a timely manner, see *EEOC v. Commercial Office Prod. Co.*, 486 U.S. 107 (1988).

138. 29 C.F.R. § 1601.13.

139. 42 U.S.C. § 2000e-5(e)(2).

140. 29 C.F.R. § 1601.14; 42 *U.S.C.* § 2000e-5(b).

141. 29 C.F.R. § 1601.15.

142. 29 C.F.R. §§ 1601.15 & 1601.16.

143. 29 C.F.R. § 1601.24; 42 U.S.C. § 2000e-5.

144. 29 C.F.R. § 1601.26.

145. 29 C.F.R. § 1601.24.

146. See, e.g., *EEOC v. Mississippi Baptist Hosp.*, No. J75-228 (S.D. Miss. 1976) (unpublished); *EEOC v. Safeway Stores*, 714 F.2d 567 (5th Cir. 1983), cert. denied, 467 U.S. 1204 (1984).

147. 29 C.F.R. § 1601.25.

148. 29 C.F.R. §§ 1601.19 & 1601.28.

149. 42 U.S.C. § 2000e-5(f)(1).

150. See, e.g., *Jones v. Cross Hosp.*, 64 F.R.D. 586 (D. Md. 1974).

151. 42 U.S.C. § 2000e-5(g).

152. *Albemarle Paper Co. v. Moody*, 422 U.S. 405 (1975).

153. *Albemarle Paper Co. v. Moody*, 422 U.S. 405 (1975).

154. *Ford Motor Co. v. EEOC*, 458 U.S. 219 (1982).

155. 42 U.S.C. § 2000e-12(b); *Albemarle Paper Co. v. Moody*, 422 U.S. 405 (1975).

156. *Albemarle Paper Co. v. Moody*, 422 U.S. 405 (1975).

157. 42 *U.S.C.* § 2000e-5(k).

158. *Robinson v. Lorillard Corp.*, 444 F.2d 791 (4th Cir. 1971).

159. *Christiansburg Garment Co. v. EEOC*, 434 U.S. 412 (1978).

160. *Quiroga v. Hasbro, Inc.*, 943 F.2d 346 (3d Cir. 1991), cert. denied, 502 U.S. 940 (1991).

161. 42 U.S.C. § 1981a.

162. 42 U.S.C. § 1981a. *Compare Humphrey v. Southwestern Portland Cement Co.*, 369 F. Supp. 832 (W.D. Tex. 1973) (compensatory damages allowed), rev'd on other grounds, 488 F.2d 691 (5th Cir. 1974), with *Attkisson v. Bridgeport Brass Co.*, No. IP71-C-27 (S.D. Ind. 1972) (unpublished) (compensatory damages not allowed).

163. *Tomka v. Seiler Corp.*, 66 F.3d 1295 (2d Cir. 1995).

164. See, e.g., *Jones v. Continental Corp.*, 789 F.2d 1225 (6th Cir. 1986).

165. *Carter v. Lutheran Medical Ctr.*, 879 F. Supp. 94 (E.D. Mo. 1995), appeal dismissed, 87 F.3d 1025 (8th Cir. 1996).

166. 42 U.S.C. § 2000e-2(e).

167. 42 U.S.C. § 2000e-2(h).

168. *International Bhd. of Teamsters v. United States*, 431 U.S. 324 (1977).

169. *American Tobacco Co. v. Patterson*, 456 U.S. 63 (1982).

170. *Albemarle Paper Co. v. Moody*, 422 U.S. 405 (1975).

171. 41 C.F.R. §§ 60-3.1 through 60-3.18.

172. 41 C.F.R. § 60-3.1(A).

173. 42 U.S.C. § 2000e-5(e)(2).

174. 42 U.S.C. § 2000e-10.

175. 42 U.S.C. § 2000e-8(c).

176. 29 C.F.R. § 1602.7.

177. 29 C.F.R. § 1602.8; 18 U.S.C. § 1001.

178. 29 C.F.R. § 1602.11.

179. 29 C.F.R. § 1602.13.

180. 29 C.F.R. § 1602.14.

181. 29 U.S.C. § 206(d).

182. *Howard v. Ward County*, 418 F. Supp. 494 (D.N.D. 1976).

183. *Usery v. Allegheny County Sch. Dist.*, 544 F.2d 148 (3d Cir. 1976), cert. denied, 430 U.S. 946 (1977); *Usery v. Charleston County Sch. Dist.*, 558 F.2d 1169 (4th Cir. 1977); *Pearce v. Wichita County*, 590 F.2d 128 (5th Cir. 1979); *Marshall v. Owensboro-Daviess County Hosp.*, 581 F.2d 116 (6th Cir. 1978); *Marshall v. City of Sheboygan*, 577 F.2d 1 (7th Cir. 1978).

184. 29 U.S.C. § 213(a)(1).

185. 29 U.S.C. § 206(d)(1).

186. 29 U.S.C. § 206(d)(1).

187. *Brennan v. City Stores, Inc.*, 479 F.2d 235 (5th Cir. 1973). See also *Marcoux v. Maine*, 797 F.2d 1100 (1st Cir. 1986).

188. 29 C.F.R. § 1620.13(a).

189. 29 C.F.R. § 1620.13(e).

190. *Hodgson v. Golden Isles Convalescent Homes*, 468 F.2d 1256 (5th Cir. 1972).

191. 29 C.F.R. § 1620.15.

192. 29 C.F.R. § 1620.16(a).

193. 29 C.F.R. § 1620.17(a).

194. 29 U.S.C. § 206(d)(1).

195. See, e.g., *Hodgson v. Golden Isles Convalescent Homes*, 468 F.2d 1256 (5th Cir. 1972); *Hodgson v. Kuakini Hosp.*, No. 71-3322 (D. Haw. 1973) (unpublished); *Hodgson v. Good Shepherd Hosp.*, 327 F. Supp. 143 (E.D. Tex. 1971); *Shultz v. Royal Glades, Inc.*, No. 70-356-CIV-PF (S.D. Fla. 1971) (unpublished).

196. See, e.g., *Brennan v. St. Luke Hosp.*, No. 1737 (E.D. Ky. 1973); *Hodgson v. Cook*, No. 71-2045 (C.D. Cal. 1972).

197. See, e.g., *Hodgson v. Skyvue Terrace, Inc.*, No. 70-1168 (W.D. Pa. 1972) (unpublished); *Hodgson v. Brookhaven Gen. Hosp.*, 436 F.2d 719 (5th Cir. 1970).

198. See, e.g., *Marshall v. Edward J. Meyer Memorial Hosp.*, No. 71-453E (W.D.N.Y. 1982) (unpublished); *EEOC v. Central Kan. Medical Ctr.*, 705 F.2d 1270 (10th Cir. 1983).

199. See, e.g., *EEOC v. Mercy Hosp. & Medical Ctr.*, 709 F.2d 1195 (7th Cir. 1983).

200. *Beall v. Curtis*, 603 F. Supp. 1563 (M.D. Ga. 1985).

201. *Gunther v. County of Wash.*, 623 F.2d 1303 (9th Cir. 1980), aff'd, 452 U.S. 161 (1981); *Lemons v. City & County of Denver*, 620 F.2d 228 (10th Cir.), cert. denied, 449 U.S. 888 (1980).

202. *International Union of Elec., Radio & Mach. Workers v. Westinghouse Elec. Corp.*, 631 F.2d 1094 (3d Cir. 1980), cert. denied, 452 U.S. 967 (1981). See also *Lemons v. City & County of Denver*, 620 F.2d 228 (10th Cir.), cert. denied, 449 U.S. 888 (1980).

203. *AFSCME v. State of Wash.*, 770 F.2d 1401 (9th Cir. 1985).

204. 29 C.F.R. § 1620.11.

205. *City of Los Angeles v. Manhart*, 435 U.S. 702 (1978).

206. *Arizona Governing Comm. v. Norris*, 463 U.S. 1073 (1983).

207. 29 U.S.C. § 206(d)(1).

208. 29 C.F.R. § 800.148, no longer effective as of August 20, 1986, per 51 Fed. Reg. 29,816 (1986).

209. 29 C.F.R. § 800.148; *Construction and Application of Provisions of Equal Pay Act of 1963* (29 U.S.C. § 206(d)) *Prohibiting Wage Discrimination on the Basis of Sex,* 7 A.L.R. Fed. 707.

210. 29 C.F.R. § 1620.26.

211. 29 U.S.C. § 206(d)(1); 29 C.F.R. § 1620.25.

212. 29 C.F.R. § 1620.33.

213. 29 C.F.R. § 1620.33.

214 *Bartlett v. The Public Health Trust of Dade County, Florida,* No. 95-1724 (S.D.Fla. 1996) (unpublished).

215. 29 U.S.C. §§ 621 through 634.

216. 29 U.S.C. § 621(b).

217. 29 U.S.C. § 623(f)(2)(B).

218. 29 U.S.C. § 631.

219. *EEOC v. Cosmair, Inc.,* 821 F.2d 1085 (5th Cir. 1987).

220. 29 U.S.C. § 626(f).

221. 29 U.S.C. § 630(b) (definition of employer).

222. 29 U.S.C. § 663a was added to cover discrimination by the federal government. The Civil Service Commission was given administrative responsibility for handling the complaints of federal employees and job applicants.

223. *EEOC v. Wyoming,* 460 U.S. 226 (1983). See also *Kelly v. Wauconda Park Dist.,* 801 F.2d 269 (7th Cir. 1986), cert. denied, 480 U.S. 940 (1987).

224. 29 U.S.C. §§ 623(b) & (c).

225. 29 U.S.C. § 623(a).

226. 29 U.S.C. § 623(d).

227. 29 U.S.C. § 623(e).

228. 29 C.F.R. § 1625.4(b).

229. 29 U.S.C. § 630(1).

230. *Public Employees Retirement Sys. of Ohio v. Betts,* 492 U.S. 158 (1989).

231. 29 U.S.C. § 623(f)(2)(B).

232. 29 U.S.C. § 626(f).

233. *Hazen Paper Co. v. Biggins,* 507 U.S. 604 (1993).

234. 29 U.S.C. § 623(f)(1).

235. 29 U.S.C. § 623(f)(1).

236. 29 U.S.C. § 623(f)(2)(A).

237. 29 U.S.C. § 623(f)(2).

238. 29 U.S.C. § 631(c)(1); 29 C.F.R. § 1625.12(a).

239. 29 C.F.R. § 1625.13.

240. *Scharon v. St. Luke's Episcopal Presbyterian Hosps.,* 929 F.2d 360 (8th Cir. 1991).

241. *Lukaszewski v. Nazareth Hosp.,* 764 F. Supp. 57 (E.D. Pa. 1991).

242. 29 U.S.C. § 626(b).

243. 29 U.S.C. § 626(b).

244. *Hazen Paper Co. v. Biggins,* 508 U.S. 948 (1993).

245. 29 U.S.C. § 626(b). There are separate procedural rules for federal employees who allege ADEA violations. 29 U.S.C. § 633a.

246. 29 U.S.C. § 626(e).

247. 29 U.S.C. § 626(d).

248. At least one circuit court of appeals has held that, where the basic purposes of the notice requirement were met by providing the EEOC an opportunity to conciliate the complaint while it was fresh and the defendant received early notice of a possible lawsuit, equitable consideration permitted the plaintiff to bring suit. *Dartt v. Shell Oil Co.*, 539 F.2d 1256 (10th Cir. 1976), aff'd, 434 U.S. 99 (1977).

249. 29 U.S.C. § 626(d).

250. 29 U.S.C. § 626(d).

251. 29 U.S.C. § 633(b).

252. 29 U.S.C. § 626(d).

253. *EEOC v. Clay Printing Co.*, 13 F.3d 813 (4th Cir. 1994).

254. See *EEOC v. Corry Jamestown Corp.*, 719 F.2d 1219 (3d Cir. 1983) (EEOC entitled to a jury trial when bringing an action under the ADEA on behalf of an aggrieved individual). See also *Steck v. Smith Barney, Harris Upham & Co., Inc.*, 661 F. Supp. 543 (D.N.J. 1987) (claim brought under the ADEA is not arbitrable despite an agreement to arbitrate disputes that arise out of the termination of employment).

255. 29 C.F.R. § 1627.3.

256. *O'Connor v. Consolidated Coin Caterers Corp.*, 116 S. Ct. 1307 (U.S. 1996).

257. *Crawford v. Medina Gen. Hosp.*, 96 F.3d 830 (6th Cir. 1996).

258. 29 U.S.C. §§ 794 through 794d. The Vocational Rehabilitation Act is also known as the Rehabilitation Act and the Rehab Act. The original statute referred to "handicapped individuals" rather than "individuals with disabilities." Thus, court opinions interpreting the Act, as well as federal regulations, may use the term "handicap," rather than "disability." Both terms are used interchangeably here. Legal researchers should concentrate on both terms.

259. This section is often referred to by its section number from the original bill (503), but is codified at 29 U.S.C. § 793.

260. This section is often referred to by its section number from the original bill (504), but is codified at 29 U.S.C. § 794.

261. 29 U.S.C. § 794.

262. See, e.g., *United States v. Baylor Univ. Medical Ctr.*, 736 F.2d 1039 (5th Cir. 1984), cert. denied, 469 U.S. 1189 (1985); *United States v. University Hosp.*, 575 F. Supp. 607 (E.D.N.Y. 1983), aff'd, 729 F.2d 144 (2d Cir. 1984). But see *Trageser v. Libbie Rehabilitation Ctr.*, 462 F. Supp. 424 (E.D. Va. 1977), aff'd, 590 F.2d 87 (4th Cir. 1978), cert. denied, 442 U.S. 947 (1979).

263. Pub. L. 100-259, amending 29 U.S.C. § 794.

264. *Leckelt v. Board of Comm'rs of Hosp. Dist. No. 1*, 909 F.2d 820 (5th Cir. 1990) (employee who refused to reveal human immunodeficiency virus (HIV) test results); *Aikins v. St. Helena Hosp.*, 843 F. Supp. 1329 (N.D. Cal. 1994) (patient's wife may sue hospital with inadequate deaf interpreter services).

265. Pub. L. 100-259, amending 29 U.S.C. § 794.

266. Regulations interpreting the Rehabilitation Act have been issued by both the Department of Labor and the Department of Health and Human Services. The Department of Labor regulations appear at 29 C.F.R. §§ 32.1 through 32.51. The Health and Human Services regulations, cited throughout this chapter, appear at 45 C.F.R. §§ 84.1 through 84.61.

267. 29 U.S.C. § 706(8)(b).

278. 45 C.F.R. § 84.3(j)(2)(i).

269. 45 C.F.R. § 84.3(j)(2)(iii).

270. 45 C.F.R. § 84.3(j)(2)(iv).

271. *Cook v. Rhode Island*, 10 F.3d 17 (1st Cir. 1993).

272. 45 C.F.R. § 84.3(k).

273. *Jackson v. Veterans Admin.*, 22 F.3d 277 (11th Cir. 1994).

274. *Guice-Mills v. Kerwinski*, 967 F.2d 794 (2d Cir. 1992).

275. See also *Klein v. Manor Healthcare*, 19 F.3d 1433 (6th Cir. 1994) (physical therapist with erratic behavior due to brain cancer not "otherwise qualified" to work at a health care facility).

276. 29 U.S.C. § 706(8)(C).

277. *School Bd. of Nassau County v. Arline*, 480 U.S. 273 (1987).

278. *Doe v. Centinela Hosp.*, No. CV 87-2514 PAR (C.D. Cal. July 7, 1988) (unpublished).

279. *Leckelt v. Board of Comm'rs*, 714 F. Supp. 1377 (E.D. La. 1989).

280. *Leckelt v. Board of Comm'rs*, 909 F.2d 820 (5th Cir. 1990).

281. *Roth v. Lutheran Gen. Hosp.*, 57 F.3d 1446 (7th Cir. 1995).

282. *Doe v. Alliquippa Hosp. Ass'n.*, Civ. No. 93-570 (W.D. Pa. Sept. 29, 1994) (unpublished).

283. *Johnson v. New York Hosp.*, 96 F.3d 33 (2d Cir. 1996).

284. *Mauro v. Borgess Medical Ctr.*, 886 F. Supp. 1349 (W.D. Mich. 1995).

285. See *Smith v. Administrator of Veterans Affairs*, No. CV 79-3726-RMT (Px) (C.D. Cal. 1983) (unpublished) (discharge of nurse because of epilepsy violated Section 504); *Doe v. Region 13 Mental Health-Mental Retardation Comm'n.*, 704 F.2d 1402 (5th Cir. 1983) (mentally ill psychiatric therapist not qualified to continue at mental health center because of suicidal tendencies).

286. 45 C.F.R. § 84.1.

287. *Hurley-Bardige v. Brown*, 900 F. Supp. 567 (D. Mass. 1995).

288. 45 C.F.R. § 84.3(k).

289. 45 C.F.R. § 84.12.

290. 45 C.F.R. § 84.12.

291. *Coffman v. West Virginia Bd. of Regents*, 386 S.E.2d 1 (W. Va. 1988).

292. *Southeastern Community College v. Davis*, 442 U.S. 397 (1979). See also *School Bd. of Nassau County v. Arline*, 480 U.S. 273 (1987).

293. *Bradley v. University of Tex. M.D. Anderson Cancer Ctr.*, 3 F.3d 922 (5th Cir. 1993), cert. denied, 510 U.S. 1119 (1994).

294. In re *Westchester County Medical Ctr.*, No. 91-504-2 (HHS App. Bd., Apr. 20, 1992) (unreported).

295. 45 C.F.R. § 84.14.

296. 45 C.F.R. § 84.13.

297. 45 C.F.R. § 84.14.

298. 45 C.F.R. § 84.14.

299. 45 C.F.R. § 84, app. A, ¶ 4.

300. 45 C.F.R. § 84.5.

301. 45 C.F.R. § 84.6(c).

302. 45 C.F.R. § 84.6(c).

303. 45 C.F.R. § 84.7.

304. 45 C.F.R. § 84.8(a).

305. 45 C.F.R. § 84.10.

306. 29 C.F.R. §§ 1640.1 through 1640.13.

307. 29 C.F.R. § 1640.1.

308. 29 C.F.R. § 1640.6(c)(2).

309. 29 C.F.R. § 1640.6(c)(2).

310. 29 C.F.R. § 1640.10(a).

311. 29 C.F.R. § 1640.10(b).

312. 41 C.F.R. § 60-741.28(c).

313. *Kedra v. Nazareth Hosp.*, 868 F. Supp. 733 (E.D. Pa. 1994).

314. See, e.g., *Pandazides v. Virginia Bd. of Educ.*, 13 F.3d 823 (4th Cir. 1994) (compensatory damages permitted); *Rodgers v. Magnet Cove Pub. Schs.*, 34 F.3d 642 (8th Cir. 1994) (compensatory damages permitted); cf. *EEOC v. AIC Sec. Investigations, Ltd.*, 55 F.3d 1276 (7th Cir. 1995) (compensatory and punitive damages permitted under the ADA).

315. See *Waldrop v. Southern Co. Servs.*, 24 F.3d 152 (11th Cir. 1994).

316. 42 U.S.C. §§ 12101 through 12213.

317. 42 U.S.C. § 12102(2).

318. 29 C.F.R. § 1630, Appendix.

319. 42 U.S.C. § 12114.

320. 42 U.S.C. § 12112.

321. 42 U.S.C. § 12111(5).

322. 42 U.S.C. §§ 12112(b) & 12113.

323. 42 U.S.C. §§ 12111(9) & (10).

324. 42 U.S.C. § 12111(9).

325. *EEOC Compliance Manual*, No. 915.002 (Mar. 14, 1995).

326. *McDonald v. Pennsylvania*, 62 F.3d 92 (3d Cir. 1995).

327. *Krauel v. Iowa Methodist Med. Ctr.*, 95 F.3d 674 (8th Cir. 1996).

328. But see *Pacourek v. Inland Steel*, 916 F. Supp. 797 (N.D. Ill. 1996) (holding that infertility constitutes a disability under the ADA).

329. *Shafer v. Preston Mem'l Hosp. Corp.*, 107 F.3d 274 (4th Cir. 1997).

330. *EEOC Enforcement Guidance on Americans with Disabilities Act and Psychiatric Disabilities*, No. 915.002 (Mar. 25, 1997).

331. *EEOC Compliance Manual*, No. 915.002, Section 902 (Mar. 14, 1995).

332. *Harris v. H&W Contracting Co.*, 102 F.3d 516 (11th Cir. 1996); *Sicard v. Sioux City*, 950 F. Supp. 1420 (N.D. Iowa 1996).

333. *Murphy v. United Parcel Serv.*, 946 F. Supp. 872 (D. Kan. 1996).

334. *Runnebaum v. NationsBank of Md.*, 123 F.3d 156 (4th Cir. 1997).

335. 29 C.F.R. § 1630.2(m).
336. 29 C.F.R. § 1630.3.
337. 29 C.F.R. § 1630.4(2).
338. 29 C.F.R. Pt. 1630, Appendix.
339. *Johnson v. Children's Hosp.*, Civ. No. 94-5698 (E.D. Pa. June 5, 1995) (unpublished), affirmed without opinion, 79 F.3d 1138 (3d Cir. 1996).
340. *McDaniel v. Mississippi Baptist Med. Ctr.*, 877 F. Supp. 321 (S.D. Miss.), aff'd without opinion, 74 F.3d 1328 (5th Cir. 1995).
341. 29 C.F.R. Pt. 1630, Appendix.
342. 29 C.F.R. § 1630.2(o).
343. 29 C.F.R. Pt. 1630, Appendix.
344. *Schmidt v. Methodist Hosp.*, 89 F.3d 342 (7th Cir. 1996).
345. *Despears v. Milwaukee County*, 63 F.3d 635 (7th Cir. 1995).
346. *Eckles v. Consolidated Rail Corp.*, 94 F.3d 1041 (7th Cir. 1996).
347. *Hudson v. MCI Tele. Corp.*, 87 F.3d 1167 (10th Cir. 1996).
348. *Kocsis v. Multi-Care Mgmt.*, 97 F.3d 876 (6th Cir. 1996).
349. *Aka v. Washington Hosp. Ctr.*, 116 F.3d 876 (D.C. Cir. 1997).
350. *Deane v. Pocono Med. Ctr.*, No. 96-7174 (3d Cir. Aug. 25, 1997) (unpublished).
351. *EEOC Enforcement Guidance on Pre-Employment Inquiries under the Americans with Disabilities Act* (May 19, 1994).
352. *EEOC Interim Enforcement Guidance on the Application of the ADA of 1990 to Disability-Based Dysfunctions in Employer Provider Health Insurance* (June 8, 1993).
353. 42 U.S.C. § 12201(c); 29 C.F.R. § 1630.16(f).
354. *Gonzales v. Garner Food Serv., Inc.*, 89 F.3d 1523 (11th Cir. 1996).
355. See also *EEOC v. CNA Ins. Cos.*, 96 F.3d 1039 (7th Cir. 1996) (holding that an employee on full disability benefits is not otherwise qualified for employment under the ADA).
356. *Parker v. Metropolitan Life Ins. Co.*, 121 F.3d 1006 (6th Cir. 1997) (en banc).
357. *Anderson v. Gus Mayer Boston Store*, 924 F. Supp. 763 (E.D. Tex. 1996).
358. *Pappas v. Bethesda Hosp. Ass'n.*, 861 F. Supp. 616 (S.D. Ohio 1994).
359. 42 U.S.C. § 12188.
360. 42 U.S.C. § 12188.
361. *Hogan v. Bangor & Aroostook R.R. Co.*, 61 F.3d 1034 (1st Cir. 1995).
362. See, e.g., *Miller v. Maxwell's Int'l Corp.*, 991 F.2d 583 (9th Cir. 1993), cert denied, 510 U.S. 1109 (1994).
363. See, e.g., *Jones v. Continental Corp.*, 789 F.2d 1225 (6th Cir. 1986).
364. *EEOC v. AIC Sec. Investigations, Ltd.*, 55 F.3d 1276 (7th Cir. 1995).
365. See also *Mason v. Stallings*, 83 F.3d 1007 (11th Cir. 1996) (ADA does not provide for individual liability); *Romand v. Zimmerman*, 881 F. Supp. 806 (N.D.N.Y. 1995) (hospital personnel director and chief executive officer cannot be liable under the ADA and the Rehabilitation Act). But see *Jendusa v. Cancer Treatment Ctrs.*, 868 F. Supp. 1006 (N.D. Ill. 1994) (finding individual liability under ADA).

366. 42 U.S.C. §§ 1981 through 1981a, 2000e through 2000e-16, & 12209; 2 U.S.C. §§ 1201 through 1224.

367. *Wards Cove Packing Co. v. Atonio*, 490 U.S. 642 (1989).

368. 42 U.S.C. §§ 2000e-2(k) through (n); 42 U.S.C. § 12112.

369. *Price Waterhouse v. Hopkins*, 490 U.S. 228 (1989).

370. 42 U.S.C. § 2000e-2(m).

371. *Lorance v. AT&T*, 490 U.S. 900 (1989).

372. 42 U.S.C. § 2000e-5(e).

373. *Patterson v. McLean Credit Union*, 491 U.S. 164 (1989).

374. 42 U.S.C. § 1981.

375. 42 U.S.C. § 1981a.

376. 42 U.S.C. § 1981a.

377. 42 U.S.C. § 1981a.

378. 42 U.S.C. § 1981.

379. 42 U.S.C. § 1981.

380. *EEOC Notice of Policy Guidance on Application of Damage Provisions of the Civil Rights Act of 1991* (Dec. 27, 1991).

381. *Rivers v. Roadway Express*, 511 U.S. 298 (1994). See also *Landgraf v. USI Film Prods.*, 511 U.S. 244 (1994).

382. *Patterson v. McLean Credit Union*, 491 U.S. 164 (1989).

383. 29 U.S.C. §§ 2601 through 2654.

384. 29 U.S.C. § 2611(4) (definition of employer); 5 U.S.C. § 6381 (civil servants).

385. 29 C.F.R. § 825.700.

386. 29 U.S.C. § 2612(a).

387. 29 U.S.C. § 2612(a).

388. 29 U.S.C. § 2611(2).

389. 29 U.S.C. § 2614.

390. 29 U.S.C. § 2614.

391. 29 C.F.R. §§ 825.100 through 825.702.

392. 29 C.F.R. § 825.114.

393. 29 C.F.R. § 825.200.

394. 29 C.F.R. § 825.203.

395. 29 C.F.R. §§ 825.100 through 825.800.

396. *Hott v. VDO Yazaki Corp.*, 922 F. Supp. 1114 (W.D. Va. 1996).

397 *Bauer v. Dayton-Walther Corp.*, 910 F. Supp. 306 (E.D. Ky. 1996).

398. *Oswalt v. Sara Lee Corp.*, 74 F.3d 91 (5th Cir. 1996).

399. *Brannon v. Oshkosh B'Gosh, Inc.*, 897 F. Supp. 1028 (M.D. Tenn. 1995).

400. *Sakellarion v. Judge & Dolph, Ltd.*, 893 F. Supp. 800 (N.D. Ill. 1995).

401. *Seidle v. Provident Mut. Life Ins. Co.*, 871 F. Supp. 238 (E.D. Pa. 1994).

402. 29 C.F.R. § 825.207(d).

403. 29 C.F.R. § 825.220(d).

404. *EEOC's Enforcement Guidance: Workers' Compensation and the ADA* (September 2, 1996).

405. 29 C.F.R. § 1630.2(p).

406. *Hudson v. MCI Tele. Corp.*, 87 F.3d 1167 (10th Cir. 1996).

407. *EEOC Enforcement Guidance on the Effect of Representations Made in Application for Benefits on the Determination of Whether a Person Is a "Qualified Individual with a Disability" Under the Americans with Disabilities Act of 1990*, No 915.002 (Feb. 12, 1997).

408. *McNemar v. Disney Store*, 91 F.3d 610 (3d Cir. 1996), cert. denied 117 S. Ct. 958 (1997).

409. See also *Kennedy v. Applause, Inc.*, 90 F.3d 1477 (9th Cir. 1996); *Budd v. ADT Sec. Sys., Inc.*, 103 F.3d 699 (8th Cir. 1996).

410. *Mohamed v. Marriott Int'l, Inc.*, 944 F. Supp. 277 (S.D.N.Y. 1996).

411. *Simon v. Safelite Glass Corp.*, 943 F. Supp. 261 (E.D.N.Y 1996).

412. *Rissetto v. Plumbers & Steamfitters Local 343*, 94 F.3d 597 (9th Cir. 1996).

413. *Prynder v. Tractor Supply Co.*, 109 F.3d 354 (7th Cir. 1997).

414. *Rivera-Flores v. Bristol-Myers Squibb Caribbean*, 112 F.3d 9 (1st Cir. 1997).

415. *Patterson v. Tenet Healthcare, Inc.*, 113 F.3d 343 (8th Cir. 1997).

416. *O'Neil v. Hilton Head Hosp.*, 115 F.3d 272 (4th Cir. 1997).

417. *Cole v. Burns Int'l Sec. Servs.*, 105 F.3d 1465 (D.C. Cir. 1997).

Index

A

Acquired immunodeficiency syndrome, capped insurance benefits for, Americans with Disabilities Act of 1990, 81

Addiction, to drug, former, as disability, 70–71

Adverse impact theory, Civil Rights Act of 1964, employment discrimination, 3–4

Advertising, discrimination based on sex, 9–10

After childbirth, employment of women after, discrimination based on sex, 9

Age Discrimination in Employment Act, 44–52

employee benefit plans, 49

enforcement, 49–51

exceptions, exemptions, 48–49

bona fide occupational qualification, 48

bona fide seniority systems, 49

reasonable factors other than age, 48

forty years of age, employee over, discrimination against, 44–52

prohibited acts, 45–48

recordkeeping requirements, 51–52

remedies, 49–51

retirement ages, mandatory, 49

subterfuge, meaning of, 47

AIDS. *See* Acquired immuno-deficiency syndrome

Albemarle Paper Co. v. Moody, significance of, 33

Alcohol use, as disability, 56

American Tobacco Co. v. Patterson, significance of, 36

Americans with Disabilities Act of 1990, 67–86

application questions, 79–80

Attorney General, federal court action filed by, 84

compensatory damages, 84

disability, defined, 68–70

drug addiction, former, as disability, 70–71

enforcement, 83–86

human immunodeficiency virus, asymptomatic, as disability, 73

impairment, defined, 69

injunctive relief, compensatory damages, 84

insurance, 80–83

Americans with Disabilities Act of
1990—*continued*
  acquired immunodeficiency
    syndrome, capped benefits
    for, 81
  subterfuge, 81
  interview questions, 79–80
  investigation, by Equal Employ-
    ment Opportunity Commission,
    83
  major life activities, defined,
    69–70
  medication, disability controlled
    with, 72
  otherwise qualified,
    determination, 73
    recent developments, 73–75
    two-step process, 73
  psychological impairment, 71
  reasonable accommodations, 75–78
    "materially adverse" employ-
      ment action, 77
    socializing, areas allocated for,
      making accessible, 76
  regarded as having impairment,
    defined, 70
  remedies, 83–86
  respondeat superior liability,
    imposition of, 85
  substantially limiting, defined, 69
Apprenticeship program, admission
  into, 2
*Arizona Governing Committee v.
  Norris*, significance of, 42
Attorney General, federal court
  action filed by, Americans with
  Disabilities Act of 1990, 84
Attorneys' fees, Civil Rights Act of
  1964, 33–34

B

Back pay awards, Civil Rights Act of
  1964, 33

Behavioral manifestations of
  handicap, 64–69
BFOQ. *See* Bona fide occupational
  qualification
Bona fide occupational qualification
  age discrimination and, 48
  Civil Rights Act of 1964, 35
  sex as, 8
Bonus plans, sexual discrimination
  and, 11

C

Childbirth, discrimination
  regarding, 12–16, 23–24
City of Los Angeles v. Manhart,
  significance of, 42
Civil Rights Act of 1964, 1–37
  adverse impact theory, employ-
    ment discrimination, 3–4
  Albemarle Paper Co. v. Moody,
    significance of, 33
  American Tobacco Co. v. Patterson,
    significance of, 36
  apprenticeship program,
    admission into, 2
  attorneys' fees, 33–34
  back pay awards, 33
  bona fide occupational
    qualification, 35
  color, race, discrimination based
    on, distinguished, 5
  compensatory damages, 34
  conciliation, by Equal
    Employment Opportunity
    Commission, 32
  consent degree, 34
  continuing violation doctrine, 36
  defenses, available to employer,
    35–36
  disparate impact theory, employ-
    ment discrimination, 3–4
  disparate treatment theory, em-
    ployment discrimination, 2–3

enforcement, 31–35
Equal Employment Opportunity
    Commission, filing complaint
    with, 31
Equal Pay Act of 1963,
    relationship, 10–11
International Brotherhood of Team-
    sters v. United States, significance
    of, 35
investigation, by Equal Employ-
    ment Opportunity Commission,
    32
national origin, discrimination
    based on, 28–30
    tests in English, to non-English
        speaking pool, 28
notice, 36–37
    posting of, in conspicuous place,
        36
personal liability, employer, 34
punitive damages, 34
race, discrimination based on, 4–7
    business necessity, facially
        neutral action, 5
    color, distinguished, 5
    disparate impact, personnel
        policies, 6
    hospital, policies with discrimi-
        natory effect, 5–7
    Thirteenth Amendment, crimi-
        nal litigation, 7
recordkeeping, 36–37
    on employee racial, ethnic iden-
        tity, 37
religion, discrimination based on,
    26–28
    reasonable accommodation,
        religious expression, while
        at work, 27–28
    Trans World Airlines, Inc. v.
        Hardison, significance of, 27
remedies, 31–35
reporting, 36–37
retaliation provision, 4

reverse discrimination, 30–31
    preferential hiring, 30
    Weber v. Kaiser Aluminum &
        Chemical Corp., significance
        of, 30
right to sue letter, 32
seniority arrangements, 35
sex, discrimination based on, 8–25
    abortion, employees right to,
        23–24
    accident insurance, 11
    advertising, 9–10
    after childbirth, employment of
        women after, 9
    bona fide occupational qualifica-
        tion, sex as, 8
    bonus plans, leave, 11
    childbirth, 12–16, 23–24
    comparable worth theory, 10–11
    dress code policies, 16
    effeminate male, refusal to hire,
        16
    employer liability, 20–23
    employment opportunity
        columns, 9–10
    Equal Pay Act of 1963,
        relationship, 10–11
    Family and Medical Leave Act of
        1993, 15
    family-oriented questions,
        asking job applicant, 10
    fringe benefits, 11–12
    grooming, 16
    haircuts, requirements
        regarding, 16
    hospital benefits, 11
    human immunodeficiency
        virus-positive patient,
        refusal to treat, 24
    International Union v. Johnson
        Controls, Inc., significance
        of, 12–13
    leave, 11
    life insurance, 11

Civil Rights Act of 1964—*continued*
  medical benefits, 11
  *Newport News Shipbuilding & Dry
    Dock Co. v. EEOC,*
    significance of, 15
  preemployment inquiries, 9–10
  pregnancy, 12–16, 23–24
    employment of women
      during, 9
    no disability per se, 14–15
    temporary disability due to,
      firing of employee, 14
  profit sharing plan, 11
  psychological injury, caused
    by hostile work
    environment, 18
  retirement benefits, 11
  same-gender sexual harassment,
    24–25
  scope of impermissible behavior,
    20–23
  sex change operation, employee
    planning to have, discharge
    of, 16
  sexual harassment, 17–20
    hostile environment
      harassment, 17–18
    quid pro quo, 17–18
    types of, 17–18
  sexual orientation, 16
  supervisor, liability of, 20
  ties, requirement of, 16
  *United Auto Workers v. Johnson
    Controls,* significance of, 13
  unwed mother, decision not to
    hire, 13
state fair employment practice
  agency, attempt to resolve
  dispute, 31
statute of limitations, 36
tests, professionally developed,
  use of, 36
training program, admission
  into, 2

unlawful employment practices, 2
Civil Rights Act of 1991, 86–88
Color, race, discrimination based on,
  distinguished, 5
Comparable worth
  Equal Pay Act of 1963, 41
  evaluation, vs. competitive
    market, 41
  theory of, 10–11
Compensation, discrimination and,
  46
Competitive market, vs. comparable
  worth evaluation, 41
Conciliation, by Equal Employment
  Opportunity Commission, Civil
  Rights Act of 1964, 32
Conflict of laws, 91–95
  disability definitions, conflicting,
    93–95
  leave, 92–93
Consent degree, Civil Rights Act of
  1964, 34
Contagious diseases, as disability,
  56–57
Continuing violation doctrine, Civil
  Rights Act of 1964, 36
Cosmetic disfigurement, as
  disability, 54

D

Disability
  application questions, about
    applicant's, 64–65
  behavioral manifestations of, 64–69
  defined, 53–60, 68–70
Discrimination based on sex, abortion, employee's right to, 23–24
Disparate impact theory, employment discrimination, 3–4
Disparate treatment theory, employment discrimination, 2–3
Dress code policies, discrimination
  based on sex and, 16

Drugs. *See also* Medication
  addiction to, former, as disability,
    70–71
  use of, as disability, 56

E

Employee benefit plans, Age
  Discrimination in Employment
  Act, 49
Employee waivers of discrimination
  claims, 95–97
Employment opportunity columns,
  discrimination based on sex and,
  9–10
English, tests in, to non-English
  speaking pool, national origin,
  discrimination based on, 28
Equal conditions, usage of term,
  Equal Pay Act, 39
Equal employment opportunity
  laws, overview, 1
Equal Employment Opportunity
  Commission, filing complaint
  with, Civil Rights Act of 1964, 31
Equal Pay Act of 1963, 37–44
  accident insurance, 41
  *Arizona Governing Committee v.
    Norris*, significance of, 42
  City of Los Angeles v. Manhart,
    significance of, 42
  Civil Rights Act of 1964,
    relationship, 10–11
  comparable worth, 41
  competitive market, vs. compara-
    ble worth evaluation, 41
  defenses, available to employer,
    42–43
  enforcement, 43–44
  equal conditions, usage of term, 39
  equal pay standard, 38–39
  equal work, defined, 38–39
  fringe benefits, 41–42
  hospital benefits, 41

hospital employees, 39–41
  leave, 42
  life insurance, 41
  medical benefits, 41
  profit sharing plan, 42
  red circle rates, 43
  remedies, 43–44
  retirements benefits, 42
  similar working conditions, usage
    of term, 39
Equal pay standard, 38–39
Equal work, defined, 38–39
Evaluation, comparable worth, *vs.*
  competitive market, 41

F

Family-oriented questions, asking
  job applicant, sex discrimination
  and, 10
Financial assistance, federal, employer recipients of, Rehabilitation
  Act of 1973, 53
Forty years of age, employee over,
  discrimination against, 44–52
Fringe benefits
  discrimination based on sex,
    11–12
  Equal Pay Act of 1963, 41–42

G

Gender, discrimination based on. *See*
  Sex
Government contractors, Rehabilita-
  tion Act of 1973, 53
Graves' disease, as disability, 72
Grooming, employment require-
  ments regarding, 16

H

Haircuts, employment requirements
  regarding, 16

HIV. *See* Human immunodeficiency virus

Homosexuality, sexual discrimination and, 16

Hospital benefits
Equal Pay Act, 41
sexual discrimination and, 11

Hospital employees, Equal Pay Act of 1963, 39–41

Hostile environment sexual harassment, 17–18

Human immunodeficiency virus
asymptomatic, as disability, 73
as disability, 57
patient with, refusal to treat, 24
test results, refusal to divulge, 57

I

Impairment, defined, 69

Insurance benefits
Americans with Disabilities Act of 1990, 80–83
capped, acquired immunodeficiency syndrome, 81
subterfuge, 81

International Brotherhood of Teamsters v. United States, significance of, 35

International Union v. Johnson Controls, Inc., significance of, 12–13

Interview questions, 64–65, 79–80

Investigation, by Equal Employment Opportunity Commission, 83
Civil Rights Act of 1964, 32

L

Learning disability, 54

Leave benefits
Equal Pay Act, 42
sexual discrimination and, 11

Lorance v. AT&T, 86
significance of, 86

M

Major life activities, defined, 69–70

Medical benefits
Equal Pay Act, 41
sexual discrimination and, 11

Medical Leave Act, 88–91

Medication, disabilities, controlled with, 72

Mental illness, employment discrimination and, 54

Mental retardation, employment discrimination and, 54

Morbid obesity, employment discrimination and, 54

N

National origin, discrimination based on, 28–30
tests in English, to non-English speaking pool, 28

Nearsightedness, as disability, 72

Newport News Shipbuilding & Dry Dock Co. v. EEOC, significance of, 15

Notice to employees
Civil Rights Act of 1964, 36–37
posting of, in conspicuous place, 36

O

Obesity, morbid, employment discrimination and, 54

"Otherwise qualified," determination of, 73
recent developments, 73–75
two-step process, 73

P

Patterson v. McLean Credit Union
significance of, 86

Personal liability, of employer, Civil Rights Act of 1964, 34
Preemployment inquiries, sexual discrimination and, 9–10
Pregnancy, sexual discrimination and, 12–16, 23–24
employment of women during, 9
no disability per se, 14–15
temporary disability due to, firing of employee, 14
Price Waterhouse v. Hopkins
significance of, 86
Profit sharing plan
Equal Pay Act, 42
sexual discrimination and, 11
Psychological impairment, as disability, 71
Psychological injury, caused by hostile work environment, sexual discrimination and, 18

Q

Quid pro quo sexual harassment, 17–18

R

Race, discrimination based on, 4–7
business necessity, facially neutral action, 5
color, distinguished, 5
disparate impact, personnel policies, 6
hospital, policies with discriminatory effect, 5–7
Thirteenth Amendment, criminal litigation, 7
Reasonable accommodations of disability, 61–63, 75–78
example of, 61–62
"materially adverse" employment action, 77

socializing, areas allocated for, making accessible, 76
Recordkeeping requirements
Age Discrimination in Employment Act, 51–52
Civil Rights Act of 1964, 36–37
on employee racial, ethnic identity, 37
Rehabilitation Act of 1973, 65–66
Red circle rates, 43
"Regarded as having impairment," defined, 70
Rehabilitation Act of 1973, 52–67
accommodation, reasonable, 61–63
example of, 61–62
alcohol, 56
application questions, about applicant's handicap, 64–65
behavioral manifestations of handicap, 64–69
compensatory damages, right to, 67
contagious diseases, 56–57
cosmetic disfigurement, 54
disability, defined, 53–60
drugs, 56
enforcement, 66–67
financial assistance, federal, employer recipients of, 53
government contractors, 53
human immunodeficiency virus, 57
test results, refusal to divulge, 57
interview questions, about applicant's handicap, 64–65
learning disability, 54
mental illness, 54
mental retardation, 54
notice, 65–66
obesity, morbid, 54
otherwise qualified, 55–56
defined, 55
punitive damages, right to, 67
recordkeeping, 65–66

Rehabilitation Act of 1973—*continued*
remedies, 66–67
reporting, 65–66
Section 504, 60–61
self-evaluation requirement, 65
*Southeastern Community College v.
Davis*, significance of, 62
tuberculosis, 56–57
Religion, discrimination based on,
Civil Rights Act of 1964, 26–28
reasonable accommodation,
religious expression, while at
work, 27–28
*Trans World Airlines, Inc. v.
Hardison*, significance of, 27
Reporting, Civil Rights Act of 1964,
36–37
Respondeat superior liability, imposi-
tion of, under Americans with
Disabilities Act of 1990, 85
Retaliation provision, Civil Rights
Act of 1964, 4
Retirement ages, mandatory, 49
Retirement benefits
caused by hostile work
environment, 11
Equal Pay Act and, 42
Reverse discrimination, 30–31
Civil Rights Act of 1964, 30–31
preferential hiring, 30
*Weber v. Kaiser Aluminum &
Chemical Corp.*, significance of,
30
Right to sue letter, Civil Rights Act of
1964, 32

S

Same-gender sexual harassment,
24–25
Self-evaluation requirement, of
disability, 65
Seniority systems, 35
bona fide, 49

Seventy years of age, employee under, discrimination against, 44–52
Sex, discrimination based on, 8–25
abortion, employee's right to,
23–24
accident insurance, 11
advertising, 9–10
after childbirth, employment of
women after, 9
bona fide occupational qualification, sex as, 8
bonus plans, leave, 11
childbirth, 12–16, 23–24
comparable worth theory, 10–11
dress code policies, 16
effeminate male, refusal to hire, 16
employer liability, 20–23
employment opportunity
columns, 9–10
Equal Pay Act of 1963,
relationship, 10–11
Family and Medical Leave Act of
1993, 15
family-oriented questions, asking
job applicant, 10
fringe benefits, 11–12
grooming, 16
haircuts, requirements regarding,
16
hospital benefits, 11
human immunodeficiency virus-
positive patient, refusal to treat,
24
*International Union v. Johnson Con-
trols, Inc.*, significance of, 12–13
leave, 11
life insurance, 11
medical benefits, 11
*Newport News Shipbuilding & Dry
Dock Co. v. EEOC*, significance
of, 15
preemployment inquiries, 9–10
pregnancy, 12–16, 23–24
employment of women during, 9

no disability per se, 14–15
temporary disability due to, firing of employee, 14
profit sharing plan, 11
psychological injury, caused by hostile work environment, 18
retirement benefits, 11
same-gender sexual harassment, 24–25
scope of impermissible behavior, 20–23
sex change operation, employee planning to have, discharge of, 16
sexual harassment, 17–20
hostile environment harassment, 17–18
quid pro quo, 17–18
types of, 17–18
sexual orientation, 16
supervisor, liability of, 20
ties, requirement of, 16
United Auto Workers v. Johnson Controls, significance of, 13
unwed mother, decision not to hire, 13
Sex change operation, employee planning to have, discharge of, 16
Sexual harassment
discrimination based on sex, 17–20
hostile environment harassment, 17–18
quid pro quo, 17–18
types of, 17–18
Sexual orientation, sexual discrimination and, 16
Similar working conditions, usage of term, 39
Southeastern Community College v. Davis, significance of, 62
State fair employment practice agency, attempt to resolve dispute, Civil Rights Act of 1964, 31

Statute of limitations, Civil Rights Act of 1964, 36
Substantially limiting, defined, under Americans with Disabilities Act of 1990, 69
Subterfuge
under Age Discrimination in Employment Act, 47
under Americans with Disabilities Act of 1990, 81
Supervisor, liability of, sexual discrimination, 20

T

Tests, professionally developed, use of, Civil Rights Act of 1964, 36
Tests in English, to non-English speaking pool, national origin, discrimination based on, 28
Ties, requirement of, 16
Training program, admission into, 2
Trans World Airlines, Inc. v. Hardison, significance of, 27
Tuberculosis, as disability, 56–57

U

United Auto Workers v. Johnson Controls, significance of, 13
Unlawful employment practices, Civil Rights Act of 1964, 2
Unwed mother, decision not to hire, sexual discrimination, 13

W

Waivers of discrimination claims, 95–97
Wards Cove Packing Co. v. Atonio, significance of, 86
Weber v. Kaiser Aluminum & Chemical Corp., significance of, 30